The Unifying Theory of Everything

The Unifying Theory of Everything

Koran & Nature's Testimony

Second Edition

Muhammed A. Asadi

Writers Club Press
New York   Lincoln   Shanghai

The Unifying Theory of Everything
Koran & Nature's Testimony

All Rights Reserved © 2000 by Muhammed A. Asadi

No part of this book may be reproduced or transmitted in any form or by any means, graphic, electronic, or mechanical, including photocopying, recording, taping, or by any information storage retrieval system, without the written permission of the publisher.

Writers Club Press
an imprint of iUniverse, Inc.

For information address:
iUniverse
2021 Pine Lake Road, Suite 100
Lincoln, NE 68512
www.iuniverse.com

ISBN: 0-595-12904-8

Printed in the United States of America

"If we do discover a complete theory, it should in time be understandable in broad principle by everyone, not just a few scientists. Then we shall all, philosophers, scientists and just ordinary people, be able to take part in the discussion of why it is that we and the Universe exist. If we find the answer to that, it would be the ultimate triumph of human reason—for then we would truly know the <u>mind of God</u>."
(Stephen W. Hawking, *A Brief History of Time*, 1988)

"…The <u>nature of God</u>, according to which he has originated humankind. There is no changing the order that God has established. That indeed is the standard established order (<u>deen al qiyyam</u>). But most among humankind understand not
(Koran 30:30)

INTRODUCTION

"And We have indeed made the Koran easy for learning and remembrance. Then is there any who will learn from it?"
(Koran 54: 17, 22, 32, 40)

I remember sitting on the big recliner in the guestroom of my grandparent's house, with the Koran (Qur'an) sitting on my lap. I had recently discovered several translations of the book in my father's closet. Coming from a fairly religious family background, I had been taught about the basics of traditional Islam and about the Koran being a revered, Holy Book, which only a few could grasp in knowledge and understanding. The contents of the Book were thus always a mystery to me. By discovering these translations, I had unlocked the cave of wonders, so to speak.

I had expected to find magical material in the Koran. What I knew of religion, in the society that I grew up in, was mostly magic and awesome miracles cloaked in a few sprinklings of logical arguments. In the weeks and the many years to follow, I was to discover otherwise.

One of the first things that strikes any reader of the Koran is its simplicity of expression and consistency. The thoughts are laid out one by one; they overlap bearing no temporal limitations, due to the unique nature of the book, contrary to books produced by human minds. It is here that people get confused and give up on the Book. Once you get a grasp of this trend in the Koran, its consistency of words and thoughts, you see a unity not seen in any book produced by the human mind, any that I have read at least. This aspect of the Koran stunned me very early on as I progressed in my reading.

I was 13 when I first discovered the Koran in English. Part of my motivation to read it was to get some "spiritual" benefits that I was told its reading would bring, rather than any lesson or meaning that might be useful. I remember reading it everyday, ten pages, fifteen, and twenty. It amazed me. I was in the eighth grade then and was very interested in biology, having aspirations of becoming a doctor someday. I was surprised at all the references to the creation of man, the animals, the flight of birds, aging and death and the predictions about people's psychology and behavior, all linked to an understanding of God and his message for humanity. It made a lot of sense to me. It was as if the book was "speaking" to me. The ideas were simple to understand, and as I discovered later on, very powerful and challenging, considering the time they were penned down. It was after those few initial verses (ayah) that amazed me, that I realized that to fully understand the wonders of this book; I needed to study what the experts were saying about natural processes discussed in the Koran. This book was not magic. It was simple, straightforward and to the point. Somehow it communicated with me unlike any book that I had read before.

I remember one day at school being puzzled by a remark my Biology teacher made when someone asked him to link the Koran with what we were learning about human reproduction in class. He remarked, " Religion and science are two separate things which should never be brought together, they are meant to be apart. It is not right to try to mix them." He then proceeded to quote something from Bertrand Russell's book, *Why I am Not a Christian*, about how the Bible says something about the hare, chewing cud when in reality it does not.

I asked myself that day, just as I ask people today who make such a comment: If you believe as a premise that God made us, then He should know His creation. If you believe that the Koran is God's word then when it discusses human creation or reproduction or any other natural phenomena, it should not make errors. Simple straightforward logic demands that. Do not say that the Koran cannot contain scientific facts and then also say, in the same breath, that it came from the maker of all things. Of course, I also add today, that the Bible is not the same thing as the Koran, neither do the two have the same author.

In 1986 my father started getting seriously ill with Motor Neuron Disease. He was getting slowly paralyzed, so I had to sit long hours with him to make sure that he didn't hurt himself or fall down. I remember doing a lot of reading in those long hours and with that reading I made a lot of connections in my mind. I read through multiple versions of the Bible, biographies of Jesus and Muhammed, translations of the Koran and studies on comparative religion. That period was really a blessing in disguise for me even though I did a lot of complaining. It was during those days that I discovered Maurice Bucaille's book titled, The Bible, The Koran and Science (1982). This became the foundation work for me in my studies on linking of scientific facts with description of natural phenomena found in the Koran.

How a French surgeon, a complete stranger to the Koran, could on his first reading see that something amazing was going on in the book, similar to what I had discovered as a young teenager, seemed too much of a coincidence to me. I took Bucaille's work and built upon it. I expanded it to include the social sciences and social issues based on empirical social research done by professionals. My previous writings, *Koran: A Scientific Analysis (1992)* and *The Message of Islam and the Qur'an (1995)* reflect some of that work.

In 1990, I transcribed in booklet form, a video lecture titled, *The Amazing Qur'an* [delivered by a Canadian Mathematician, Gary Miller]. That lecture had a profound impact on me. For the first time to my knowledge, the Koran was presented as a theory that offered falsification, a truly scientific theory. My initial publication of five hundred copies at an obscure printing press, sold out in a couple of months. The booklet became well known all through the Islamic world and went through three separate publications in the first year. It made its way to a publishing company in Saudi Arabia and from there it reached Gary

Miller in Canada. Now, it is well known all through the Islamic world and has inspired numerous web sites. The chapter in this book, *Scientific Revelation*, is modeled after that booklet.

As my reading of the Koran continued, I was discovering for myself the amazing nature of the Book. I was hearing opinions that people have and have had about God and society, and I was thinking and reasoning with myself. I was well aware of the skepticism that people have and that I had, consciously or unconsciously about God and religion. That idea of rejection is always there, waiting for an opportunity to confront us and demand an answer, at the worst possible moment, be it a moment of joy or sorrow. It is within all of us, the suggestions of *Shaitan*, the culturally inspired rebel "inside" every person. Whatever you want to call it, be it the whispers of the Id, according to Freud, or the suggestions of *Shaitan*, according to the Koran, is it not true that all of us have been confronted by thoughts of denying at one time or the other?

I know of people who would not read the Koran for the very reason that this idea of denying God would find grounds to stick in their minds, as they think the book will be primitive nonsense. They think that they will find some mythical religious "mumbo jumbo" in the Koran, which will fuel their skeptical side, and so they will become irreligious. They want to protect their belief by covering up anything that might give an edge to their skeptical side. What they are unaware of though, is that if they take that route they do not have any certain confirmation to start with, the type of confirmation demanded by the Koran, which can result only by verification through certain knowledge, given how our mind works. Mere drugging yourself with "blind faith" based religion, according to Marx "opium of the masses," does little for personal or human welfare.

History bears witness to the destruction caused in the name of "faith" based religion. It is for this reason that the Koran shows us the "outside", it shows us the facts and then brings us home to a sound conclusion as to why confirmation is the only reasonable option. Belief, according to the Koran, should be based upon reason (4:82, 3:195 etc); it is arrived at scientifically by facts provided by nature and the natural world. The Koran provides meaningful connections to that end.

Believing in God as a reality can never come through blind-faith unless you "kill" your mind either through drugging yourself or such rigorous programming that all alternative thoughts are filtered by internalized "faith" criteria before they enter your mind. Those internalized "faith" criteria might be contradictory or belong to any system, but they get accepted without reason nonetheless. How is "blind faith" in Christianity truer than "blind faith" in Hinduism or Islam? That is a legitimate question that the proponents of "blind faith" have no answer for.

We need to think and reason to confirm, to be sure even of our experiences. Are not dreams the most "real" experience when we are having them, how "real" are they in reality? I have "seen" the fulfillment of all possible "dreams" that anyone can have in my dreams, according to Freud, "wish fulfillment." Love, career, fame, all has been mine in my dreams; yet when I woke up, reality hit me in the face.

Considering all the efforts people put into useless things, given the transitory nature of this existence, seems so irrational yet people are so programmed that they do not give it a second thought. What is termed "important" in the popular culture, has been so internalized that it becomes "natural" as a mode of thinking and behavior. Everything else is seen as weird and people following different paths to the path in vogue, are termed "losers". Who are the real losers though, objectively speaking?—That question is what the Koran efficiently answers based on a logical framework, empirical evidence, falsification and an extremely parsimonious rendition.

I sit while typing this introduction in the university computer lab and I can see panicking students run all over the place, trying to complete their term papers. They are getting ready for "judgment day", the day when their grades will be announced. Soon, there will be new faces, new people running around in the same manner, trying to fulfill the obligations that the "market" has laid out for them. For a few, their work will remain in this world as literary contributions, to be used by all, regardless of market value. For others, their comfortable or not so comfortable life will end and if they could look back at it, they would surely say, just as we sometimes say about the parts of our lives that are over, "It was short, I should have planned better."

I remember learning more from a comment my first semester psychology professor made, in a fleeting moment, than I did in all the classes that semester. She said, "We seek to "kill" time, yet how limited is the time that we seek to "kill"! My sincere hope is that we all, of whatever race, gender, nationality or religion, learn from our experiences that have "died" already and make the effort to reach the destiny that is decreed for us, to which nature and the natural world bears witness.

I need to add a special thanks to a few people who have helped and supported my effort all along. First, to my mother, whose support and encouragement helped make the publication of my second book possible and provided motivation for this work. My friend in Pakistan, Naveed Nasim, whose relentless efforts made the publication of my first book, *Koran: A Scientific Analysis (1992),* and Gary Miller's *Amazing Qur'an* (1990) a successful reality. A special thanks to my brothers Ghias Asadi and Ahmed Asadi for their support. My friend and brother Aybars Kahyaoglu deserves special thanks for supporting me in days of extreme opposition in Springfield, Missouri. And an extra thanks to Aybars for reminding me of Ibraheem's (Abraham) sacrifice during difficult times. Mohammed Shaikh, a friend, and a scholar of the Koran, deserves special thanks for opening my eyes to certain areas of the Koran. Special thanks goes to all those who have contributed through encouragement or criticism to this effort, especially through all the feedback I received from my web page at http://www.rationalreality.com

Muhammed A. Asadi
August 16, 1999.
Chicago, Illinois.
(Revised, December 2002)

SCIENTIFIC REVELATION KORAN & CRITICAL RATIONALISM

"Say: What thing is greatest in testimony? Say: God is witness between you and I, and that this Koran has been inspired in me that I many warn with it you and whomsoever it be conveyed to..." (Koran 6:19)

Religion throughout the history of humankind has had a tremendous hold on humanity. According to Emile Durkheim, the French Sociologist, the first organized institutions of mankind were religious in character. Even today, religion is of primary importance to millions of individuals who try to live by it and give it a special place in their lives. Therefore any issue involving religion in our world is worthy of discussion. Science, in its popular usage, is generally defined as the systematic observation of natural phenomena and their workings. Since the industrial revolution, it is seen as the driving force behind all human progress in the future. Those who fail to apply its methodology to their lives are kept at the lowest strata of society in today's highly competitive world. As both science and religion are widespread in the modern world, each having dogmatic believers, antagonism has resulted. The common notion in the culture being that science and religion are opposites; i.e. they repel each other as like poles of a magnet.

2 / The Unifying Theory of Everything

According to the sociologist Max Weber, in his article, *Science as a Vocation*, science has resulted in the "disenchantment" of the world. The "enchantment" of the world was due to, according to him, people relying on religion and giving magical explanations to perfectly logical, natural phenomena.

This chapter attempts to use the Koran to examine Max Weber's claims about religion. The source of Islam is a book, just one book, the Koran. Modern Islam however, has added other sources, which the Koran does not validate. The Koran, is historically the earliest written text we possess in the the Arabic language and as such is the only valid authority on Islam as conveyed by the prophet Muhammed. The other sources, *Hadith* and *Fiqh*, date from over 200 years after Muhammed's death. I will therefore not deal with these other sources as they do not represent the "original" Islam, so to speak.

Within its text, the Koran names itself many times as a book revealed directly by God, in which God is speaking in the first person. The Koran, says that true believers, *"reason about the origin of the heavens and the earth (Koran 3:190-191)."* This itself is science by definition when done in a systematic way. By doing such, a person gets to the truth by discovering the "nature of God" [His *Sunna*—in Arabic], as reflected by his creation and confirmed by His revelation the Koran. Thus contrary to the concept of a "supernatural", the Koran talks about nature and creation being an expression of God's attributes. We can look inside the *"Mind of God"* so to speak by studying his creation.

Arthur J Arberry, in the introduction to his translation of the Koran states, *"The Koran is a book apart.."* The Koran, in its contents and presentation is indeed a book apart. The unique thing about the Koran, given the time of its origin is that it does not contain any scientific inaccuracies or errors. Such errors would have been unavoidable if the Koran had a human origin. Not only that, the Koran preempts many of today's hard earned scientific facts. Facts that just a hundred years back would have been impossible to discover. We possess written documents of the Koran going back at least fourteen centuries.

The scientific system of inquiry is emphasized time and again in the Koran. The linking of science and rationality with the verses of the Koran is not only legitimized but also encouraged by God in the Koran. The Koran tells the reader that if he or she does not know something or are unsure that they should ask "those who are informed" (people having information, 25:59). In the case of all the scientific and natural phenomena discussed in the Koran, the people having knowledge and information would most definitely be the scientists. Thus the Koran discourages unreasoned belief.

A critical and scientific analysis of the Koran is encouraged by the Koran in this statement:

> *"Do they not carefully consider the Koran. If it had been from anyone other than God, they would have found in it many contradictions." (Koran 4:82)*

If the Koran is indeed the word of the creator, then it must be error-free when it discusses details about proven facts of science, like description of stages in embryology. This is exactly the attitude reflected in the Koran's presentation. For example, the details about embryology in the Koran are presented in a fashion that would facilitate belief only after those verses have been checked by known findings. They are presented as a challenge:

> *"If you are in doubt then (consider this).... (22:5 etc)"*

The same is also witnessed throughout the Koran when the book makes statements like, *"Do you not know.... (Or) Have you not seen and considered, etc."* Also consider all the falsification tests contained in the Koran, like the one which challenges people to produce a chapter comparable to the Book. All these legitimize and encourage a rational/scientific inquiry into the truthfulness of the Koran.

Maurice Bucaille, who was one of the first researchers to popularize the linking of the Koran and Science, in his best selling books, *The Bible, the Quran and Science*, and *What is the Origin of Man?*, demonstrated that given the history of the origin of the Koran, it could not have been the work of a man or group of men living in Arabia or anywhere else at that time. Lecturing at the French Academy of Medicine, he concluded on the subject:

> *"It makes us deem it quite unthinkable for a man of Muhammed's time to have been the author of such statements on account of the state of knowledge in his day. Such considerations are what give the Koranic revelation its unique place and forces the impartial scientist to admit his inability to provide an explanation which calls solely on materialistic reasoning."(Bucaille 1985)*

Keith L. Moore, head of the department of anatomy, at the University of Toronto, was shown verses of the Koran dealing with the microscopic stages of the human embryo. He was so surprised at what he found that he went back and revised the history of embryology in his standard texts on the subject. The books that Keith L. Moore authored are used at prestigious institutions like Yale and all around the world. He stated concerning the issue:

> *"It is clear to me that these statements (in the Koran on embryology) must have come to Muhammad from God. This proves to me that Muhammed must have been the messenger of God or Allah." (Rehaili 1995)*

Professor Marshall Johnson, surprised at what the Koran had to say on geology, sates:

> *"There is nothing here in conflict with the concept that divine intervention was involved in what he (Muhammed) was able to say." (Rehaili 1995)*

Bertrand Russell, the famous English philosopher and celebrated agnostic, in his book, *Religion and Science*, states, *" I cannot admit any method of arriving at the truth except that of science"* (page, 18). That is the method that I use throughout this study, and the end conclusion is an arrival at truth.

The Koran claims to originate with the one (God) who originated everything (Koran 55:2). Therefore, we have every right to logically inquire if the originator of the earth and the heavens, in the knowledge that he gives us about them knows what we have discovered about their origin through modern science.

The Koran exists in the world today. Therefore, if we do not accept the book's claim of being a revelation, then we must come up with an explanation as to its origin. The existence of the Koran cannot be denied; we have a problem, which demands an explanation to justify denial, if denial were our choice.

People who reject the Koran's claim of originating with an all-knowing God, have come up with explanations and theories as to the origin of the Koran. No matter what the details of the particular theory might be, they all, throughout the ages, basically reduce to two hypotheses:

i) *Muhammad was a liar.* He got his information from the outside and presented it to people as a revelation from God. The proponents of this hypothesis claim that Muhammad who "borrowed" information from other sources, composed the Koran. Some even suggest that Muhammad was helped by a "group" of people to compose the Koran.

ii) *Muhammad was a deluded:* The second hypothesis suggests that Muhammed was deceived or deluded in that he believed that he was a prophet when in fact he was not. To the people who offer this hypothesis, the Koran is the product of the "deluded" mind of Muhammed. Muhammad's hallucinations.

It may sound surprising but the book that is being attacked, the Koran, is also well aware of these two hypothesis that people have been presenting throughout the ages in trying to reject it:

Hypothesis 1 suggests that Muhammad was a liar. The Koran states:

> "They (the rejecters) say: 'These are tales of the ancients, which he has caused to be written down so that they are <u>dictated to him</u> morning and evening."
> (Koran 5:25)

Hypothesis 2 suggests that Muhammed was self-deceived. The Koran states:

> "The ones who reject almost trip you up by glaring at you when they hear The Reminder (Koran), and they say,' He is indeed <u>deranged</u>."(Koran 68:51)

Most people, who present these in the form of theories, are forced to take them together in conjunction. Logically speaking however, both these hypothesis are mutually exclusive and cannot be taken together. They can stand on their own, if facts support them, but taken together they collapse. For example, if a man is a liar (Hypothesis 1) then when someone asks the man a question, he has to search for the answer. He looks either within himself for the answer or asks his friends in secrecy so that he can give the inquirer a satisfactory response. He knows that he is not a prophet so he has to lie to convince the questioner. On the other hand, if the man is deluded (Hypothesis 2) then when someone asks the man a question, he does not search for the answer, if he does not know it. He is deluded, self-deceived, he believes he is a prophet and the answer will be given to him by revelation. A large section of the Koran came as answers to questions that people would ask.

To repeat the above, if the man is a liar, he knows he is not a prophet and investigation can provide evidence as to where the material came from, but if he is deluded, even though the material presented is his own hallucinations, still he cannot be termed a liar for he genuinely believes he is a prophet. If a man is a liar then he is not self-deceived, if he is self-deceived then he is not a liar. Therefore Hypothesis 1 and Hypothesis 2 cannot be mixed up in explaining the Koran. However, what we see is that people need both excuses to explain certain things in the Koran. They often start by presenting Hypothesis 1 (Muhammed was a liar) and end up with Hypothesis 2 (Muhammed was self-deceived), i.e. Muhammed was a liar and self-deceived. This cannot be, logically speaking as we have seen above.

It may surprise you again that the Koran is also aware of this illogical stand that people take by terming Muhammad both a liar and self deluded. The Koran states:

> "And they have turned away and said, 'One taught (by others), <u>and</u> a madman (44:14)."

The Koran can be Hypothesis 1) The product of a liar, or Hypothesis 2) The product of a deceived mind, or it can be what it claims to be, i.e. God's revelation; <u>but</u> it can never be both Hypothesis 1 and Hypothesis 2 at the same time. Thus it becomes impossible to reject the book's claim of being from an all-knowing God.

> "And We certainly know that there are those among you who reject it (the Koran). But it is indeed a sorrow for the rejecters, for it is indeed the certain truth (Koran 69:49-51)."

Hypothesis 1 and its implications:

If the Koran is the product of a man's mind who is a "liar", who got his information from the outside and then presented it to the world as a revelation then:

1. We have to explain the *confidence* portrayed by the various statements in the Koran. A confidence that shows that whosoever is presenting this is convinced that he indeed has the truth. As examples:

—The Koran challenges people to find a mistake in the book (chapter 4, verse 82). Now only a person who is convinced about what he has can make such a claim. Do you know of any book that makes a claim that it is 100% error free? A book that says *that* "*No falsehood can ever approach it.*" The Bible never makes such a claim.

—Another example would be the invitation given to Christians who dispute with Muslims about the nature of Jesus as presented in the Koran. The verse says:

> *"Come let us call our sons and your sons...our families and your families and let us ask God to curse the ones who are lying (about the true information on Jesus)." (Koran 3:61)*

This shows that whoever is presenting this is confident and sure that he has the truth on which the challenge is based.

—Another example of this *confidence* that a liar is incapable of portraying, is the account of when the Meccans, who wanted to kill Muhammad, came unto the mouth of the cave in which he and his friend Abu-Bakr were hiding. Abu-Bakr was afraid, Muhammed told him to "relax", "God will save us," he told him. Now if the man is a liar, one who lies to convince people that he is a prophet, you might expect him to say, "Go and look for a back way out," or "lie low and be quiet." But what he actually said shows that he had no doubt that he was a prophet and that God would save them. Hypothesis 1 cannot explain the above in the Koran.

2. If the Koran is a lie, the product of a man's lying mind, how do you account for this:

The Koran claims that it contains information that was "new" to the people it was being read to. The Meccans hated Muhammad; if this statement in the Koran was not true and the information was not "new", they would have loved to point out the source. Yet they never answered this challenge to produce similar "knowledge" as the Koran (46: 4)

As proof of the above, I'll give two examples:

1. The Koran mentions the wall of *Zulqarnain*, the two-horned one. It gives a complete description of this wall and how it was built to protect a people from outside invaders (Koran 18:96-98). The Arabs had never heard of it, or what it looked like, neither had the Arab Jews nor the Arab Christians. After the death of the prophet, they were curious about this wall mentioned in the Koran. Omar the Khalif sent out travelers to verify the existence of the wall. It is in Durbent, in the former Soviet Union. It is referred to as Alexander's

wall however modern historians dispute on whether Alexander had anything to do with it.

Compare what the Koran said over fourteen centuries back, before any Arab had set foot on Derbent to what the Columbia Encyclopaedia says:

"Derbent was founded (AD 438) by the Persians as a strategic fortress at the Iron Gates. There are remains of the Caucasian Wall (also called Alexander's Wall), built by the Persians in the 6th century. as a bulwark against northern invaders. (6th Edition, 2000)."

If Muhammed was a liar, who told him about this wall thousands of miles to the east, which no one in his area knew anything about?

2. The Koran mentions a city by the name of Iram, where a prosperous people the AAD lived. It was a city of "tall pillars":

"Have you seen how your sustainer (God) dealt with the Aad people? Iram, of the lofty pillars (Koran 89:8-8)"

Until very recently no historic record existed about Iram. However in 1973, the ancient city of Ebla was excavated in Syria. While going through the tablet library of Ebla, archaeologists came across a list of cities that Ebla traded with and on that list was a city named Iram. When reporting it in the National Geographic of December 1978, the only reference to Iram they could cite other than the tablets was the Koran, chapter 89.

In 1992 using SIR-C imaging [Synthetic Aperture Radar] using the Space Shuttle, GPR [Ground Penetrating Radar] and GMT [Geophysical Diffraction Tomography], scientists discovered Iram [also called Ubar] in southern Oman, buried under 12 meters of sand. The city contained evidence of "tall pillars" exactly as mentioned in the Koran, chapter 89. The Koran described this fact over fourteen centuries back at a time when no one in the world could have had access to this city.

If Muhammad was a liar where did he get his information? He had no way of knowing the above, since the legends about *Iram* postdate the Koran.

Hypothesis 2 and its implications:

Hypothesis 2, suggests that the Koran is the product of a man's deluded mind. If the Koran is a product of a man's hallucinations then what comes out as a result are things that are in his mind. What do you think went on in Muhammed's mind? He didn't have an easy life. He was an orphan to start with, then his grandfather who looked after him died, then his uncle who adopted him. After that, his life companion, his wife died. All his children except for one daughter died in his lifetime. Does the Koran reflect any of this? It does not even mention these things at all. Yet these were the things that surely bothered him and caused him pain through his whole life, but they never show up in a book, which is said to be the product of his deluded mind! In fact, the information contained in the Koran is such that no man living anywhere in that day or age could have known.

Consider yourself living in 7th Century Arabia. Society has very little scientific knowledge. Bedouin tribalism is the "dominant feature" of the population (*The Arabs in History,* Bernard Lewis (1958), page 23). This mostly desolate area in which you live, is an "oral" culture, with a "nomadic" lifestyle. Very few people know how to read, even fewer know how to write. Myth and magic controls people's thoughts and guides their rituals. Trade routes to the north (and the resulting contact with the major Empires) have very recently been restored, after two centuries of decline and deterioration (*The Middle East: A Brief History of the Last 2,000 Years,* Bernard Lewis, 1995). How far would you go if you wanted to discover the true origin of the Universe? How much progress would you make if you wanted to uncover the origin of life?

We can move away from Arabia and scan the world scene at that period in history. Nothing in the literature of the world, including the literature of the ancient Greeks, comes even remotely close to the accuracy of statements, without error, about the natural world, contained in the Koran. In fact some of the information that we come across in the Koran was not known until about 40 years back and some of it was not known until the day it was read in the Koran by scientists just a few years ago

Consider these documented examples:

1. *The Origin of Life:*

The Koran mentions that all life "originated" from water (Koran 21:30) and that man himself is "created" of water and so are all the animals on earth (Koran 25:54, and 24:45). These statements to an Arab would have sounded atrocious in that day and age. Even today such statements in the Koran might cause you to wonder. The fact that all life originated in water is well established by the scientific community. We have evidence to support the fact that the first living beings were cyanobacteria also called blue-green algae, and they existed in water. The fact that human beings and animals are created of water is also well established since cytoplasm the basic component of "life" in any animal cell is over 80% water.

2. *Maturity:*

The Koran mentions that a human being reaches full maturity at age forty (Koran 46:15). This is a very unusual statement. Even today most people believe that full maturity is reached at puberty and laws usually put it between 18 to 21. However, the Koran is scientifically correct where even modern ideas are not accurate. If we analyze the statement psychologically and physiologically, we find is that the *"overall quantity of stored knowledge in the mind of an individual reaches a peak at age thirty-nine and after that it gradually declines."* (Arthur C. Guyton, *Physiology of the Human Body*, 6th Ed, page 207)

3. *The Female Bee:*

The Koran mentions the bee, which leaves its home in search for food, in the verses that discusses honey (Koran 16:68, 69). It uses the female verb in describing the bee, in Arabic *faslukee*. This, to the Arab, suggests that the bee, which leaves its home in search for food, is female.

Does anyone except an expert know how to differentiate between a male and a female bee? Even today, let alone Muhammad's time, we need a specialist to differentiate between a male and a female bee. The Koran is accurate when it mentions that the female bee leaves its home in search for food; the males never leave their homes for food, it is the females who have to feed them.

4. *Embryo Sex Determination:*

The Koran says that the "ejaculated drop" determines the sex of a human baby (Koran 53:45). It is common knowledge that semen is the fluid that is ejaculated by males during sexual acts. Females do not possess such "ejaculated semen."

The sex of the baby, whether it will be male or female, will indeed be determined by the 'ejaculated drop', i.e. the father's sperm, as mentioned by the Koran. It has been scientifically established only recently that the female ovum contains only X-chromosomes. If the ejaculated drop, the father's sperm bears the Y chromosome, the offspring will be male, otherwise the offspring will be female. No one living at the time of Muhammed or even Darwin for that matter had any knowledge of such genetics, foretold centuries earlier in the Koran.

5. *The Invisible Barrier:*

The Koran states that there are two seas that meet but do not intermingle because of a barrier between them (Koran 55:19-20). It is a necessity that seas intermingle through straits between them. The Koran however is aware of a very unusual phenomenon, which scientists discovered only recently. The Mediterranean and Atlantic oceans differ in their chemical and biological constitution. The French scientist Jacques Yves Cousteau conducted various undersea investigations at the Strait of Gibraltar and explaining these phenomena concluded:

> "Unexpected fresh water springs issue from the southern and northern coasts of Gibraltar. These mammoth springs gush towards each other at angles of 45 degrees forming a reciprocal dam. Due to this fact the Mediterranean and the Atlantic Oceans cannot intermingle (as quoted by Nurbaki)."

Did Muhammed do research on the chemical and biological components of seawater to discover this unusual phenomena?

6. The Gaseous Universe:

The Koran used the Arabic word *Dukhan* (Koran 41:11), which stands for smoke. A perfect analogy for gas and particles in suspension and the gasses being hot. Scientists have only very recently confirmed that the Universe was indeed, at an early stage, a gaseous mass composed of hydrogen and some helium, a big mass of hot gasses. The Koran is more accurate in describing the gasses as "smoke" rather than the word "mist" or "fog" used frequently by scientists (Rees uses the word "fog" in his book) as the gasses were hot.

The Koran used this analogy centuries before anyone in the world had any idea about helium and hydrogen, yet even today scientists use a crude form of the same analogy. The Belgian cosmologist Georges Lemaitre, lecturing in 1930, fourteen hundred years after the Koran, described this stage of cosmic evolution as: "...*The filling of the heavens with* smoke."*(Ferris, Timothy 1997:109)*

7. The Big Bang:

> "Do not the rejecters see that the skies and earth were bound together then we disunited [or separated] them (Fataq in Arabic)..." (Koran 21:30)

In the above statement, the Koran gives an accurate description of the Big Bang, a theory of the origin of the Universe widely accepted by scientists today. The Arabic word used in the Koran to signify separation is *Fataq*. It means to dis-joint or disunite. It essentially captures, in the description, "symmetry breaking" between particles and forces that modern cosmologists talk about in explaining the complexity of the Universe.

Martin Rees, who is one of the leading cosmologists in the world, states in his book, *Our Cosmic Habitat (2001)*:

> *"Our Universe may once have been squeezed to a single point, but EVERYONE whether on Earth, or Andromeda, or even on the galaxies remotest from us can EQUALLY claim to have started from that point..."* (Rees, page 55)

According to the physicist Steven Weinberg: *"There was a time in the very early Universe.... when the forces were all the same-not only mathematically the same...but ACTUALLY the same."* (Quoted by Ferris, Timothy 1997:215)

The Koran, over 14 centuries before the "Big Bang" theory was presented, confirmed the "common origin" or source of everything in the Universe. The criticism by some that it mentions the "earth" erroneously at this stage is unfounded. The Koran is merely stating that the earth and the skies had one common origin. It mirrors the statement by Martin Rees quoted above when it mentions the "common origin" of everything, including you and I, in the Universe. How do we explain this information in the Koran, if it had its origin in the mind of a 7th century man? Professor Alfred Kroner, chairman of the Department of Geology at the Institute of Geosciences, Johannes Gutenburg University, Mainz, Germany stated about this verse in the Koran:

> *"Somebody who did not know something about nuclear physics 1400 years ago could not, I think, be in a position to find out from his own mind for instance that the earth and the heavens had the same origin, or many others of the questions that we have discussed here."*(Rehaili 1995)

8. The Expanding Universe:

The Koran talks about a Universe that is continually "expanding" (Koran 51:47). The fact that the Universe is not static but in a state of expansion was discovered by the American astronomer Edwin Hubble in the late 1920s, almost 1400 years after the Koran described it. Do you know that the Universe is expanding? Can you feel or see it expanding? No, the verification of this requires specialized knowledge and instruments, which no one at the time of Muhammad had, access to. The Koran states:

> "And the sky we built it with might and We cause the 'expansion' of it (Koran 51:47)."

9. The Death of Stars:

The Koran mentions the 'death of stars' (Koran 77:7-8). Astronomers including Dr. Patterson of Southwest Missouri State are surprised at finding this information in the Koran. They know that at the time of Muhammad, people believed that once a thing was formed, it was permanent. The Koran is very accurate when it mentions dying stars. Our own sun is a dying star.

10. Black Holes:

The Koran is aware of the phenomenon of "black holes", stars that have collapsed under their intense gravitational field, so that even light cannot escape. The Koran stated over 1200 years before John Michell stated the concept in 1767, and 1400 years before John Archibald Wheeler coined the term "black hole" in 1968:

> *I swear by the sky and (the phenomena of) Tariq.*
> *And what will explain to you what Tariq is?*
> *It is a star that pierces (or makes a hole). (Koran 86:1-3)*

The Koran uses the word <u>*Thaqib*</u> in Arabic, a word that literally signifies a puncture or a minute hole. Martin Rees, states in <u>Our Cosmic Habitat (2001)</u>

> *"Space is already being <u>punctured</u> by the formation of black holes…"*
> *(Rees, page 120)*

Michael Moyer of Popular Science writes:

> *"A black hole is infinitely dense, which means that it pulls the fabric of space-time to the breaking point—creating a deep pockmark, complete with a tiny <u>rip</u> at the bottom."*
> *(http://www.popsci.com/popsci/science/article/0,12543,211498,00.html)*

Black holes are objects literally "cut off" from the rest of the Universe. The black hole is wrapped in a zone called the "event horizon". Once the event horizon is crossed, nothing can return. A camel falling into the event horizon would literally be stretched to the dimension of a yarn (Ferris, Timothy 1998:83) and can pass through the *"eye of the needle"(Koran 7:40)*.

Contrary to the New Testament, the Koran uses this terminology in relation to *"gates to the sky"*. Many physicists have conjectured about "gates" or "passages" in space being associated with black holes. Inside the "event horizon" time itself comes to a standstill. Black holes are exceedingly important to modern physics. All endeavors towards a unifying theory, relating quantum physics to general relativity have come from black hole research.

11. The Woven Sky:

> *"By the sky with all its weavings (knitting, huu-buk in Arabic)"*
> *(Koran 51:7)*.

The Koran accurately describes the sky as having "weavings", or being like a knitted fabric. Space having "weavings" ties in with String Theory in physics. It is envisioned by scientists that at the smallest Planck Scale (10^{-35} m), space-time is indeed <u>"weaved"</u> or "knitted".

Physicist Lee Smolin, in his book, *Three Roads to Quantum Gravity (2001)*, states:

> "...Space may be 'woven' from a network of loops,...just like a piece of cloth is 'woven' from a network of threads." (Smolin, page 186)

Martin Rees, states in <u>Our Cosmic Habitat(2001)</u>

> "According to our present concepts, empty space is anything but simple..., and on an even tinier scale, it may be a seething tangle of strings." (Rees, page 107)

The idea that space is not "nothing" but "something" is a 20th century discovery, i.e. over 1300 years after the Koran. The physicist Paul Davies in his book, *The Edge of Infinity (1981)*, terms it, "One of the great scientific discoveries of the twentieth century." (Davies, page18)

12. The Movement of the Sun:

> "He created the skies and the earth for truth.
> He coils the night upon the day and He coils the day upon the night"(Koran 39:5)

At a time when a geocentric cosmology was in vogue, the Koran not only corrected the erroneous notions associated with that world-view, but made clear that night and day were caused by a coiling motion. The Koran uses the arabic verb *Kawarra* which in its original usage signifies the "coiling" of a turban around the head. A perfect analogy to the movement that causes night and day, i.e. the earth's rotation.

> "He it is who has created the night and day, and the sun and the moon. They <u>all</u>, in their orbit, swim (yasbahoon)" (Koran 39:5)

To make this notion of a rotating earth causing night and day even clearer, the Koran mentions that the night "merges" into the day and day "merges" into night (Koran 3:27) and that the night and day "interchange" into each other (Koran 24:44). The above statement stated that this change is brought about by orbital motion similar to (in principle) <u>but</u> distinct from the orbital motion of the sun and the moon. "They all" says the Koran; "all" signifies night and day, the sun and the moon. The word translated "swim" above is the Arabic *Yasbahoon*. It signifies movement with one's own motion. If you refer to a man doing this on the ground, it means he is walking and not rolled by someone else.

> *"And the sun constantly journeys towards a homing place for it*
> *And for the moon We have determined phases...*
> *It is not for the sun to <u>overtake</u> the moon;*
> *neither can the night outstrip the day.*
> *And they all swim (yasbahoon) in their own orbits (Koran 36:38-40)"*

The Koran mentions the movement of the sun. The sun's movement is not something that is evident to our eyes or experience but requires specialized equipment. Modern science has found out that the sun rotates around its axis every 26 days and is continually on a journey in space towards its "homing place", the central nucleus of our galaxy, just like mentioned in the Koran (36:39), in its orbit of around 226 million miles (accurate to within 6 percent), according to Mark Reid, a Harvard-Smithsonian astronomer. Also, the Koran is known to be the first book to use the modern term "phase" (*Manazil* in Arabic) associated with the moon's appearances.

By stating that the sun is not permitted to "overtake" the moon, the Koran is making clear for astronomers, in their own terminology, that the sun and the moon are not revolving around the same object. It also makes clear that the movement that causes night and day has nothing to do with the movement of the sun and the moon. In the first part of the statement, the sun is mentioned as the one that cannot "overtake" the moon. In the second part it is the <u>night</u> that cannot "outstrip" the day. This is completely contrary to popular earth-centered (geocentric) systems, in which day and night was associated with the sun's movement (popular at the time of Muhammed).

> Simon and Jacqueline Mitton, in their book, *Invitation to Astronomy (1986);* state on page 20:
> *...a planet travels more slowly the further it is away from the sun. Thus the Earth regularly "<u>overtakes on the inside</u>", the*

planets that are further out. The <u>overtaking</u> causes the apparent backward loop in the planet's path." (Mitton 1986:20)

Not only this, the Koran completely debunks the geocentric hypothesis when it states:

By the Sun and its brightness
And by the moon when it imitates it (i.e. reflects that brightness)
And by the day which reveals it.
By the night that conceals it." (Koran 91:1-4)

The above statements of the Koran not only reveal the reflected nature of the moon's light but also debunk the erroneous claim of the geocentrists that the sun's movement causes day and night. It is the morning that "reveals" the sun and the night that "conceals" the sun, not the other way around. In other words, the sun is stationary relative to night and day. The movement that causes night and day is not the movement of the sun!

The fact that the earth, sun and moon move with their own motion is a notion that even the "father of gravity", Isaac Newton, did not fully understand. It was clarified by Einstein in 1912 (almost 1400 years after the Koran) and formed the essence of his *General Theory of Relativity*. Physicist Brian Greene, in his book, *The Elegant Universe (1999)* states on page 71:

> *…Einstein has taught us that the warping of space is gravity. The mere presence of an object with mass causes space to respond by warping. Similarly, the earth is <u>not</u> kept in orbit because the gravitational pull of some other external object guides it…Instead, Einstein showed that objects move through space along the shortest possible paths—the "easiest possible" paths or the "paths of least resistance". (Greene, Page 71)*

13. Atomism:

> "(God is) The Knower of the unapparent. Not an atom's weight in the skies or the earth, nor anything smaller than that, or larger, escapes him, but is in a clear record." (Koran 34:3)

Many centuries before Muhammad was born, there was a well-known theory of ATOMISM, advanced by the Greeks, Democritus in particular, who lived in the 4th century BC. Democritus and the people who came after him assumed that the material world is made up of tiny indivisible particles called atoms, the smallest pieces of matter, each having the same mass, the smallest unit mass possible. The Arabs used to deal in the same concept. The word in Arabic, ZARRA, most commonly meant that.

The Koran breaking with that tradition clearly states that there are things "smaller" than an atom (see Koran 34:3 above).

It was not until 1897 that the concept of the 'indivisible atom' was challenged when the English physicist J.J Thomson, working at the Cavendish Laboratory in Cambridge found ways to study bits that had been broken off atoms *(Gribbin, John 1998. The Search for Superstrings, Symmetry, and the Theory of Everything)*

14. The Roots of Mountains:

The Koran states that mountains are like "tent-pegs", i.e. they have a root extending down into the earth like "anchors" and this gives stability and balance to the earth.

> "Have we not expanded the earth and made the mountains as tent pegs" (Koran 78:6-7)
>
> " We have cast into the earth anchors lest it shake with you" (Koran 31:10 etc.)

This fact was discovered less than 150 years ago by scientists and now accepted as a fundamental law in geology, the concept of isostacy.

M. J Selby in a standard-text on the subject entitled *"Earth's Changing Surface* (Clarendon Press, Oxford 1985) states:

> "G.B Airy in 1855 suggested that the crust of the earth could be likened to rafts of timber floating on water. Thick pieces of timber float higher above the water surface than thin pieces and similarly thick sections of the earth's crust will float on a liquid or plastic substratum of greater density. Airy was suggesting that mountains have a deep root of lower density rock, which the plains lack. Four years after Airy published his work, J.H Pratt offered an alternative hypothesis…By this hypothesis, rock columns below mountains must have a lower density, because of their greater length, than shorter rock columns beneath plains. Both Airy and Pratt's hypothesis imply that surface irregularities are balanced by differences in density of rocks below the major features (mountains and plains) of the crust. This state of BALANCE is described as the concept of ISOSTACY (Selby1985:32)."

15. The Stretching Earth:

> "Have We not expanded the earth…"(Koran 78:6-7)
> "It is God who has <u>stretched out</u> (Mad-a in Arabic) the earth, AND made therein <u>mountains</u> (as anchors) and <u>rivers</u>…"(Koran 13:3)

The Koranic verse quoted above, mentions the expansion/stretching of the earth. Mentioned together with the stretching of the earth are mountains and rivers. The surface of the Earth today is very different than it once was. It is believed that all of the continents we once connected in one giant landmass, named Pangaea (a Latin word meaning "all lands").

Expansion or widening of the sea floor is one of the main reasons continental plates are always moving, a process called 'continental drift'.

Expansion is caused by an up welling of molten material through cracks, fissures, and faults in the Earth's crust.

Currently, continents drift apart at the rate of about one inch per year. The most obvious sea floor expansion in the world is taking place under the ocean between Arabia and Africa, where the two continents are drifting apart three to four times faster than any other continental plates. When expansion occurs on land rather than the seabed, an ever-widening valley is formed such as East Africa's Great Rift Valley.

Alfred Lothar, German meteorologist and explorer, first stated the idea of the expansion of the earth in 1912, fourteen centuries after the Koran. If we get a relief map that covers Utah, Nevada, and California, in the US, we will be able to see the Basin and Range Province. The Utah Geological Survey states:

> "The ranges and basins have been forming for the past 10 to 20 million years in response to east-west <u>stretching</u> of the earth's crust. Stretching creates tension that is released by slow continuous movement or sudden movement along a fault (a break in the earth's crust), which causes earthquakes. During an earthquake, the <u>mountains rise</u> while the valleys drop along the faults. The stretching continues today."
> (Utah Geological Survey, http://www.ugs.state.ut.us/education/tc/tc12-96.htm)

Not only do mountains rise due to the "stretching" of the earth, but according to simulated models of the continents, "stretching" resulted in the formation of the major rivers on earth as well, exactly as implied by the Koran.

> "In all cases the greatest stress occurred at the location of the Earth's major rivers. This development suggests that <u>the major riverbeds came into existence as a result of expansion</u> rather than random erosion. Since the continents were fixed on an expanding surface, it may be logically deduced that

expansion caused the land masses to stretch and, at the points of greatest tension, to break, thus forming the rivers."
(*The Expanded Earth*, Benchmark Publishing & Design, Windsor, Ontario, Canada,
http://www.wincom.net/earthexp/n/rivers.htm)

16. *Oceans and Internal Waves:*

"...Or (as the example of) darkness in the <u>deep ocean</u>, covered by a wave, on top of which is a wave, on top of which are clouds. <u>Darkness one on top of the other</u> (as layers)..."(Koran 24:40)

The Koran, in the verse above, stated over 1400 years ago, that there are internal waves in a deep ocean (note that internal waves are topped by surface waves which are topped by clouds). Also stated in the verse are the layers of darkness associated with the depth of the ocean. The photograph below was taken using remote sensing equipment (satellite imagery). It reveals internal waves a few kilometers east of the Strait of Gibraltar (image at rationalreality.com)

The <u>average</u> depth of the oceans is 3795 meters (12450 feet). Without protective equipment humans cannot go down below 40 meters. At 200 meters light has been successively absorbed, layer-by-layer, in all its color frequencies except blue. There is almost no light at 200 meters.(*Oceans*, Elder and Pernetta, p. 27). Internal waves in the "deep ocean" have been recognized <u>only</u> in the past two decades (now four) due to remote sensing from space platforms.

(Apel et al.*Observations of oceanic internal waves from the ERTS*, 1975; Fedorov,*Observations of oceanic internal waves from space* 1976)

Internal waves form at the interfaces between layers of different water density, which are associated with velocity shears (i.e., where the water above and below the interface is either moving in opposite directions or in the same direction at different speeds). Oscillations can occur if the water is displaced vertically resulting in internal waves.

The Koran is the first book on earth to clearly mention "internal waves" and their association with layers of darkness in a "deep ocean". This was fourteen centuries before remote sensing equipment was invented.

17, Microscopic Embryology:

The Koran is known to be the first book to give microscopic details of human embryology, hundreds of years before the discovery of the microscope! The Koran contains information on embryology, which was not discovered till about 30 years back and certain details were new even to modern scientists but were immediately confirmed as being accurate.

The Koran mentions that at a certain stage, the developing human is like "*allaqa*", a leech-like clot. If you take a microscopic picture of a human embryo of days 7-12 and place it next to a picture of a leech, they both look identical. Not only do they look the same but they function in the same way too. Just like a leech derives nourishment from its host's blood, the embryo derives nourishment from the decidua or the pregnant endometrium. These facts about the Koran are well documented and listed by Keith L. Moore in his standard textbooks on embryology, books used in medical schools all around the world.

18. Koran on Nerve Endings:

> "Indeed, those who disbelieve in our signs, we will roast them at a fire. As often as their skins are wholly burned, we will give them in exchange other skins, that they may taste the punishment (Koran 4:56)."

It is well known to specialists today that full thickness burns destroy nerve endings, so that further burning a person after that wont cause any pain. In Bailey and Love's, *Short Practice of Surgery (20th* edition), it states:

> "...Full thickness burns are relatively painless due to the destruction of nerve endings.." (Page, 149)

In order to determine full or partial thickness loss, doctors use the "pin prick" test. How such information could have been known at the time of Muhammed is baffling to people who attribute a human origin to the Koran. The Koran states clearly that people will be given a "new skin" for the purpose of pain, thereby linking skin loss with the loss of nerve endings, which cause pain.

19. Resurrection of the Dead:

> "What, does humankind think that they will be left to roam at will? Was he not a drop ejaculated? Then he was a leech-like structure. And He (God) created and formed. And made of him a pair, the male and the female. What, is He (God) then not able to quicken the dead?" Koran 65:36-40

The above verse of the Koran questions those who reject the notion of the resurrection of the dead. What is the more difficult task, that you were created from an insignificant drop, which was so small that it couldn't be seen except through a microscope, or that one day you will be formed from your remnants?

> "What, does man think that We shall not put his bones together again? Yes indeed, We are able to shape his very fingers (Koran 75:3-4)."

Russian scientists recently discussed reproducing an extinct species of elephant by use of a microscopic unit of long-dead gene material. No one in the scientific community said that it was unreasonable. Resurrection of the dead might be an unusual thing but it certainly is not unreasonable. The use of cloning techniques throws further light on the amazing nature of the Koranic verse which compares the resurrection of the dead with human development from an insignificant zygote to the fetus. Cloning provides theoretic and empirical evidence for the resurrection of the dead.

20. **The Circulation of Blood:**

> "And surely in the cattle, there is a lesson for you. We give you to drink of what is inside their bodies, from between digested food and blood, pure milk, pleasant to those who drink it (Koran 16:6)."

The above verse of the Koran calls our attention to the food distribution function of blood. It should be kept in mind that a Muslim scientist formally discovered the circulation of blood 600 years after Muhammed's death and it was made known to the West by William Harvey, 1000 years after Muhammed had died. If Muhammed was the author of the Koran how would he have known, at the time that he lived that digested food is transported via blood and then becomes the constituent of milk secreted by the mammary glands?

21. **The "Constants":**

> "Do they [the disbelievers] not see that God has subjected for them whatsoever is in the heavens and on earth?" (Koran 31:20)
> "Indeed, We have calculated for everything a set measure."(Koran54: 49)
> "The Most Merciful (God), uplifted the sky and set the balance." (Koran 55:7)

Compare these statements in the Koran to what the physicist Paul Davies writes in his book, *The Accidental Universe* (1982):

> "The numerical values that nature has assigned to the fundamental constants, such as the charge on the electron, the mass of the proton, and the Newtonian Gravitational constant, may be mysterious, but they are critically relevant to the structure of the Universe that we perceive. As more and more physical systems from nuclei to galaxies have become better understood, scientists have begun to realize that many characteristics of these systems are remarkably sensitive to the precise value of the fundamental constants. Had nature opted for a

slightly different set of numbers, the world would have been a very different place and we would not be here to see it." (Davies 1982)

At around 300,000 years after the big bang, all parts of the Universe, even separated by more than 20 times the horizon distance, and expanding in opposite directions, in causally disconnected regions (i.e.. no cause or physical effect could pass from one region to the other), began to expand with the same expansion rate and temperature.

No natural explanation exists to explain how a chaotic explosion, the big bang resulted in a uniform expansion pattern among causally disconnected regions, expanding in opposite directions. Calculations indicate that when the Universe was a trillionth of a trillionth of a trillionth second old, it consisted of 10 to the power 80 <u>causally disconnected</u> regions, and no physical effect could have traveled from one region to another and yet 300,000 years after, cosmic background radiation proves that they all started expanding with the same expansion rate and the same temperature. It was as if they acted upon uniformly communicated intelligent direction. The "Inflation" explanation implies the same, something inbuilt. Consider what the Koran says:

"…And He (God) inspired in all the heavens their mandate (Koran 41:12)."

The "Flatness" or "smoothness" of the Universe is established by modern science and leads scientists to wonder as to how a uniform distribution of matter resulted from the big bang. The Koran is aware of this and presents the "smoothness" of the Universe as a challenge to unbelievers:

"[It is God] who has created the multiple skies, one separate from the other (as layers). You cannot see any flaw in the Merciful (God's) creation. Look again, can you make out any rifts?"(Koran 67:3)

If we deny the Koran's claim of being God's revelation, we have to account for the above information, and how it made its way into the

Koran, always without error, and always accurate. Justice and truth demands that or we are fooling ourselves alone.

Falsification Tests:

The Koran offers what is not offered by religions, generally speaking. It offers what the scientific community demands before they even listen to any new theory, *falsification tests*, based on Karl Popper's *Critical Rationalism*. The Koran presents itself with tests to disprove it, if it is false.

1. The Koran in 4:82 challenges people to find a mistake or contradiction in the book and hence disqualify it, if it is indeed a lie.
2. The Koran talks about people and how they will behave. If they were to act contrary to how the Koran foretold their behavior, it would be disqualified:

> Muhammad had an uncle by the name of Abu-Lahab. This man hated Muhammad and was always strong in opposing him. Many years before the man died, the small chapter in the Koran documented his behavior, saying that he will be condemned and will never change (Koran 111:1-5). All he had to do to prove the Koran wrong was say: *"I am a Muslim, I change my behavior, your book is wrong."* Yet he never did do it, never thought of it even though he would have loved to.

3. The Koran claims that in a pluralistic society, the Christians would always treat the Muslims better than the Jews and Idolaters (Koran 5:85,86). Now scan the world scene where Jews, Christians and Muslims live together. Are the Jews closer to the Muslims or the Christians?

The only thing the Jews have to do to disprove the Koran is to band together and treat the Muslims better than the Christians do for a little while and the Koran is disproved. Yet this has not happened and given the reputation of the Koran, never will.

4. The Koran says that if it is not what it claims to be then people should produce a document comparable to the Koran (2:23 etc). Comparison

criteria would be what I have discussed earlier: i) It should contain information, which no one knows today, but will be found out tomorrow as scientifically accurate. ii) It should contain falsification tests as the Koran. iii) It should stand the test of "forgery" and "hallucination" as the Koran does. iv) It should give "sound" scientifically testable social advice as the Koran. v) Equal the Koran on literary merits. vi) Should have God speaking in the first person as the Koran does and then pass the test of inerrancy.

In the face of all the facts that the Koran provides, it is evident that it challenges human intellect and explanation and presents itself as a challenge to traditional religion and skeptical scientists. The ancient Greeks, more learned than the pre-Islamic Arabs, whenever they opined on nature made multiple errors per every accurate statement made. (http://www.perseus.tufts.edu/GreekScience/Students/Ellen/EarlyGkAstronomy.html)

The Bible made multiple errors when it talked about the natural world and the origin of the Universe (http://bible.rationalreality.com). The Koran, contrary to that, not only avoids all the errors made by pre-scientific communities prevalent at the time, it made pioneering statements about the natural world that are amazingly accurate and were not uncovered and could not have been uncovered until recently, as documented above.

There is more testable evidence of a scientific nature presented above (http://members.aol.com /masadi/sci.htm) and in the link pages to support the single hypothesis of the divine origin of the Koran, than has been presented in support of any other single hypothesis in the entire history of science. The Koran offers what has not been offered by any "religious" book: a logical framework, empirical evidence and falsification.

If we deny the Koran's claim of being a revelation, from the One who has knowledge of everything, then we have to account for the above information, and how it made its way into the Koran, always without error, and <u>always</u> accurate. Justice, truth and sincerity demands that or we fool ourselves alone.

In the light of all this, let us consider this statement that it makes:
> *"If all of humankind and other intelligent species (Jinn) were to band together to produce the like of this Koran, they would not be able to, even if they backed up each other with help and support." (Koran 17:89)*

<u>Bibliography:</u>

1. Miller, Gary. <u>*The Amazing Quran.*</u> (Video Recording, transcribed, Sept 1990, by Muhammed A. Asadi. Lahore, Pakistan).
2. Asadi, Muhammed A. 1992<u>. *Koran: A Scientific Analysis*</u>. Lahore. Pakistan.
3. Asadi, Muhammed A. 1995. <u>*The Message of Qur'an and Islam*</u>. Lahore, Pakistan: Ferozsons' Ltd.
4. Asadi, Muhammed A. 2000. <u>The Unifying Theory of Everything: Koran & Nature's Testimony</u>.Writer's Club Press. New York (FIRST EDITION).
5. <u>Koran</u>. Translated from the Arabic.
6. Bucaille, Maurice. <u>*What is the Origin of Man*</u>? 1987. Seghers, Paris.
7. Bucaille, Maurice. <u>*The Bible, the Qur'an and Science*</u>. 1985. Seghers. Paris.
8. Rehaili. Abdullah. M. <u>*This is the Truth*</u>. 1995. Riyadh. Saudi Arabia.

Other references used are narrated and acknowledged within the text, in full, for clarity.

SELF REFERENCE KORAN & KURT GODEL

"Indeed, God takes count of everything." (Koran 4:86)

There was a fundamental crisis in mathematics about a hundred years ago, a basic disturbance that affected all of logic till it was repaired. Logicians realized that for centuries they had left out the concept of "Self-Reference." For centuries, Aristotle's rule of the "Excluded Middle" had been used. This rule is a proposition that states, "Every proposition is either true or false." Somebody was smart enough to question that very proposition. What if that proposition that states that every proposition is either true or false is false? People had overlooked that for centuries. Not so the Koran. If the Koran is what it claims to be then it should be aware of Self-Reference, as applied to its own statements.

Paul Davies, professor of Mathematical Physics at the University of Adelaide in Australia, in his book, *The Mind of God (1992)*, talks about how Self-Reference shook the very foundations of logic and how it was resolved (emphasis is mine):

> *"In spite of its superficial plausibility, the formalist interpretation of mathematics received a severe blow in 1931. In that year the Austrian mathematician and logician Kurt Godel proved a sweeping theorem to the effect that mathematical statements existed for which no systematic procedure could determine whether they are either true or false.... The fact that there exist undecidable propositions in mathematics*

came as a great shock, because it seemed to undermine the entire logical foundations of the subject.

Godel's theorem springs from a constellation of paradoxes that surround the subject of Self-Reference...The great mathematician and philosopher Bertrand Russell demonstrated that the existence of such paradoxes strikes at the very heart of logic, and undermines any straightforward attempt to construct mathematics rigorously on a logical foundation. Godel went on to adapt these difficulties of Self-Reference to the subject of mathematics in a brilliant and unusual manner. He considered the relationship between the description of mathematics and the mathematics itself...In this way, logical operations about mathematics can be made to correspond to the mathematical operations themselves. And this is the essence of the self-referential character of Godel's proof. By identifying the subject with the object—mapping <u>the description of the mathematics unto the mathematics</u>—he uncovered a Russellian paradoxical loop that led directly to the inevitability of undecidable propositions." (Davies 1993:100-101)

Self-Reference takes into consideration the "use" and the "mention" of words. When you "use" a word, it is the meaning of the word that is implied. When you "mention" a word, you are talking about the word and not its meaning. Every sentence can thus talk about the words it is using or the meaning of the word. As an example: If I say, " Youth comes before manhood," it would be logically incorrect unless specified. The reason being that in the dictionary, "Manhood (the word and not its meaning)," comes before "Youth (the word)." Since the Koran talks about numerous things and uses many words sometimes repeating them many times, if the author of the Koran was a man or group of men we should find many such logical errors of Self Reference in the book. However, we find something amazing when we apply the Self-Reference check.

If I said, "*There is a mistake in the Bible,*"to Jerry Falwell or Pat Robertson, for example, they would respond emotionally, "*No there is no mistake in the Bible. Show us a mistake.*" I could logically show them a mistake in the Bible by reading a passage like, "David made a *mistake...*" See, the word "*mistake*" is in the Bible. Now if the Bible were to say, "*There is NO mistake in this book,*" it would be falsified and disproved logically, by that example. This is no trick, it involves delicate matters of logic. However, the Bible[1] never makes such a claim, but the Koran does!

> "*Do they not consider the Koran with care. If it had been from anyone other than God, it would contain many (Kathirun) contradictions (Ikhtelaafun-).*" Koran 4:82

The meaning of the statement (use of words) is clear. Considering the nature of the Book and its diverse topics and areas of discussion, if the Book had a human origin, it should be easy to find discrepancies in it. If we consider the "mention" of the words a different picture emerges. Let us see if the Koran passes its own falsification test on the criteria of "Self Reference" using the "mention" of words.

---

[1] The Bible is not free from paradoxes (contradictions) of Self-Reference. The famous *Epimenedes Paradox* is well known. Paul, writing to Titus, says about the Cretans:

> 12. <u>One of themselves,</u> even a prophet of their own said, The Cretans are <u>always</u> liars, evil beasts, slow bellies. 13. This witness <u>is true.</u>...
>
> (Titus 1:12-13—The Bible)

An analysis based on Self-Reference tells us that if the statement that Cretans are always liars is true, then since "one of themselves (a Cretan)" said this, it must be a lie, since Cretans always lie (according to the statement made). So if the statement is true then it is a lie (based on Self-Reference). Only if the statement that "Cretans are always liars" is false can this "witness" be true. So it is a paradox, a contradiction that cannot be resolved.

In the "mention" of the word contradictions (*Ikhteelafun*), the meaning that emerges is; if the book had a human origin it should contain many (*Kathirun*), *Ikhteelafun* (contradictions, the word). Many denotes more than one. To check how many times the word "*Ikhteelafun* (contradictions)" occurs in the Koran, we make use of the index of every Arabic word in the Koran. Due to the work of Faud Abd al Baqi, we possess such an index of the Koran today, titled, *Al—Moojam al Mofahris*.

The word "*Ikhteelafun* (contradictions)" is mentioned just ONCE in the whole Koran in this particular verse. Not many (*Kathirun*) times, but only once. Therefore, the author of the Koran is aware of Self-Reference.

Some people band together the last two words of this verse: Many (*Kathirun*) Contradictions (*Ikhteelafun*). Then they say see the Koran mentions the words *Ikhteelafun Kathirun* (Many Contradictions) and the verse says that if it came from other than God it would contain *Ikhteelfun Kathirun* (Many contradictions). This is a very smart move in trying to prove the Koran false but as we are going to find out, not smart enough.

People who try to disprove the Koran by taking the last two words in conjunction are implying, in the mention of words, that if the Koran contains the words "*Ikhteelafun Kathirun* (many contradictions)," it came from other than God. The statement in the Koran is not saying that. It is saying that books from other than God can contain the words "Ikhteelafun Kathirun," but so also can a book from God. Thus they fall into the famous *Fallacy of the Converse* in logic. Rain means wet streets but wet streets do not necessarily mean rain. Similarly, the Koran did not say, "If it contains *Ikhtelafun Kathirun* (many contradictions) it came from other than God." It does not say that. By banding the two words *Ikhtelafun Kathirun* (many contradictions) together, they remove the qualifier, *Kathirun* (many) which changes the statement's meaning.

Jesus is like Adam:

> "The example of Jesus with God is like that of Adam. He created him from dust and said to him, "Be," and he was." (Koran 3:59)

The meaning of the statement is clear. Jesus being born without a father is like Adam's creation. The relatively new *Mitochondrial Eve* theory of humankind's descent gives even more credibility to this comparison, as it was a woman from whom the human race descended and Jesus had a mother only, as well.

However, in the mention of words, it says that the word "Jesus (*Eesa*)," in the Koran is like the word "Adam." It is surprising to note that indeed the word "Jesus (*Eesa*)" [page 494 of the Index] in its mention in the Koran is like the mention of the word "Adam" [page 24 of the index], Both words occur in the Koran twenty five times. Not only that, it is in the same order of succession. The verse that mentions that they are like each other is the seventh time the word "Jesus" is mentioned and the seventh time "Adam" is mentioned in the Koran.

The example of a "Dog":

> "The example of him [who forsook our signs] is as the example of the dog. If you attack him he pants with his tongue out and if you leave him alone he does the same. Such is the example of <u>THE NATION THAT DENIES OUR REVELATIONS</u>...(7:176)."

The Arabic word used for dog is "*Kalb (singular)*". The word for "dog" in the singular occurs in the Koran five times. The statement, "*Nation which denies our revelations*," occurs five times in the Koran also. Chapter 7:176 is the first time the word "dog (singular)" is mentioned in the Koran (see page 614 of the above mentioned index), and the first time the statement, "The nation which denies our revelations (page 583-584 of the index)," is mentioned. Therefore the example of "The nation which denies our revelations" is as the example of a dog (*Kalb*), in the mention or words.

Not alike:

> "The blind (al-Aama) and the seeing (al-Baseer) are NOT alike. Nor are the depths of darkness (az-Zulumaat) and the light (an-Nur). Nor is the shadow (az-Zill) as the heat (al-Haroor)…(Koran 35:19-22)[2]

The word "the blind (al-*aama*)" occurs in the Koran eight times (page 488 of the index). The word used for "the seeing" above, (al-b*aseer*), occurs nine times (page 121-122 of the index). Therefore "the blind" and "the seeing" are not alike. The statement of the Koran, which mentions that "the blind" and "the seeing" are not alike is the fifth time in succession that the word "the seeing" is used in the Koran and also the fifth time in succession that the word "the blind" is used.

The word used for "the depths of darkness," (az-*Zulumat*) occurs twelve times (see page 438-439 of the index) in the Koran; the word for "the light," (an-*Nur*), occurs thirteen times (see page 725 of the index). Thus "the depths of darkness (az-*Zulumat*)," are not the same as "the light (an-*Nur*)." The other trend that we noticed above, shows up in these words too. The statement above which mentions that "the light" is not as "the depths of darkness," is the tenth time both words are used in the Koran, if we take into consideration the use of the words in successive progression in the book. Another amazing thing that we notice is that the same statement is repeated in chapter 13: 16, and the same trend emerges [which makes it impossible to be coincidence]:

> "…Say: Are the blind and the seeing equal, or are the depths of darkness equal to the light…" (Koran 13:16)

---

[2] Please make sure while checking the count in the index that you take note of the word "the". For example, "the light (an-nur)," is different from just "light (nur)." Therefore attention needs to be paid, while counting, to the "specific" or the "general" usage of the word

If we check the succession, it is the sixth time that the word "the depths of darkness (az-Zulumat)," is used and the sixth time the word "the light (an-Nur)," is used in the Koran. We can do the same with the first part that we already covered above." The blind (al-Aama)" are not as "the seeing (al-baseer)". In the verse above, chapter 13, it is the third time the word, "the blind (al-aama)" is used and the third time the word "the seeing (al-baseer),"is used [in the verse which says one is not like the other] in the Koran. In chapter 35 above we saw that it was the fifth time that both words were used in the Koran. Another trend is emerging from the above also, i.e., whenever the Koran says that something is not like the other, the positive mentioned are always one more than the negative. For example "the seeing" (+) as opposed to "the blind" (-) and "the light" (+) as opposed to the "depths of darkness" (-). As we saw above, "the seeing (al-baseer)," is mentioned nine times as opposed to the eight of "the blind (al-aama)." Similarly, "the light (an-Nur)" is mentioned thirteen times as opposed to the twelve times that "the depths of darkness (az-zulumat)," is mentioned. The above examples should be enough to confirm this amazing trend in the Koran but let us try one more. The statement above in chapter 35 continues:

"...*nor is the shadow (az-Zill) as the heat (al-Har or al-Haroor) (Koran 35:22)*"

The word used for "the shadow (az-Zill)," is mentioned in the Koran four times (see page 434 of the index) and the word "the heat (al-Har)," is mentioned three times. The statement (35:22) which mentions that "the shadow" is not as "the heat," is the third time both words "az-Zill" and "al-har" are used in the Koran.

Did the Koran fail?

"*Say: The evil (al-Khabees) and the good (at-Tayyab) are not alike...(Koran 5:100)*"

When we come to this particular statement in the Koran on dissimilarity, the items mentioned occur an equal number of times. The word "evil (*al-Khabees*)," is mentioned seven times (see page 226 of the index) and the word, "the good (at-*Tayyab*)," seven times also (see page 432). Did the Koran fail? According to our trend above, the negative (the evil) should be one less than the positive (the good). How come "the evil" is one more than what it should be?

The Koran fails only if we cut off the statement in the middle of the sentence. The verse continues:

> "*Say: The evil and the good are not alike; Even though the <u>plenty</u> of the evil amazes you. So be careful of your duty to God, O people that understand, so that you may succeed (Koran 5:100)*"

If we are careful, just like the above statement mentions, we notice that God joins together all the evil (al-K*habees*)" in the use of words, i.e. all different forms of the word and not only "the evil (al-Khabees)", in order to differentiate between evil and good. Thus "evil (al-*Khabees*)" is separated from "good (at-*Tayyab*)."

> "*That God may separate the evil from the good and place the evil (Khabees) one upon the other also heap them ALL TOGETHER...(Koran 8:37)*"

Now acting on the advice of the above verse in the "mention" of words, if we "heap together" all the "evil (*Khabees*)," in its different forms of use in the Koran, we end up with sixteen times that the word "evil" is mentioned as against seven that the word "good" is mentioned. Thus the good and the evil are not alike if we "heap them together," even though the plenty (sixteen as against seven) of the "evil" amazes us.

This itself says volumes for the inimitability of the Koran. How could a man or group of men have produced such a mathematically/logically sound book without having any formal education in logic or mathematics and without access to any computer software or indexes?

Month and Days:

In the index of the Koran (mentioned above), if we count the times the word month (*Shahr*) is mentioned, it turns out to be twelve. There are twelve "months" in the Koran. The number of times the word "day" in the singular (*Yaum or Yauma*) is mentioned turns out to be three hundred and sixty five.

This discovery in the Koran proves, as mentioned above, that the Koran cannot be the work of a man or group of men living in the Arabian Desert over fourteen hundred years back. It also provides evidence that the Koran hasn't been tampered with. The statements that mention, "this is like that," for example is the same in succession in the "mention" of words. The verse that says that "Jesus is like Adam," for example are the seventh time both Jesus is mentioned and the seventh time Adam is mentioned. If there were any tampering, in the setting of the chapters or the numbering of the verses or additions or deletions, this sequence would completely break down. However, we find no exception. Every word is accounted for and in its proper place!

Indeed, We have created everything with a measure (Koran 54:49)
With God, everything is measured (Koran 13:8)

Bibliography:

1. Asadi, Muhammed. 1992. Koran: A Scientific Analysis. Lahore, Pakistan.
2. Davies, Paul. 1993. The Mind of God. New York. Touchstone Books.
3. Miller, Gary. The Amazing Qur'an.

GOD: THE NEW SCIENTIFIC EVIDENCE

"The Universe was not made in jest but in solemn incomprehensible earnest. By a power that is unfathomably secret, and holy and fleet. There is nothing to be done about it, but ignore it or see it."
(Annie Dillard, *Pilgrim at Tinker Creek*)

The more we advance on the path of science in all directions, micro and macro, the arguments in favor of an intelligent designer become increasingly eloquent. The origin of the "laws" of nature and the precise values of the "constants", without which life could never have originated, necessitate intelligent design.

Given the exact "mix" of these "constants", we can logically deduce from inductive premises that they were "intelligently" set by one source, i.e. one God. The "oneness" of this source is observed by the uniformity in the workings of these laws of nature all through the Universe, the common origin of everything in the Universe and the blueprint of life all across the species. When analyzed simultaneously with their logical implications, the "God Hypothesis" emerges as an empirical reality, logically deduced from inductive premises that are empirically verifiable. This in essence is pure science.

The facts that nature provides, leaves the inquirer with only two options:

1) Acknowledgement of providence based upon sincerity to the principles of science, or
2) Rejection based upon dogmatism and an abandonment of the scientific system itself.

THE ORIGIN:

The Universe consists of billions of galaxies and each galaxy has a vast number of stars. To study a galaxy, scientists record light from it on a strip of film. If the galaxy is moving away from our galaxy, the lines on the spectrum will be towards the red end of the film, this is called *red shift*. By this mechanism scientists conclude that with the exception of a few nearby galaxies, all the galaxies are moving away from us, and the further away they are the faster they are moving away.

The expansion of the Universe, discussed above, began with an explosive event termed the *Big Bang*. In 1965 a type of radiation called the *Cosmic Background Radiation* was discovered (also called the microwave background radiation) by Arno Penzias and Robert Wilson. All regions of the sky send the same amount of this radiation to the earth. This was the breakthrough for the Big Bang theory. Long before 1965, scientists had predicted that we should be able to find energy remaining from the Big Bang. They had now factually confirmed the faint remnant of the energy produced during the explosive birth of the Universe. This radiation has a temperature of 3K (therefore, it is also called 3K radiation) and it is very close to the value predicted by scientists before it was discovered. It is very different to the radiation coming from a particular portion of the Universe since its intensity does not increase nor decrease by pointing an antenna but is uniform from all locations to the earth.

In 1948, the *Steady State Theory* was advanced which now has fallen out of favor by the discovery of 3K radiation and the 1992 COBE signature. Scientists today accept the Big Bang theory as being the most reliable, with the most evidence to support it. However, they do not know what caused the Big Bang nor how the Big Bang resulted in a smooth galaxy as ours. All the "laws" of nature originated at the time of the Big Bang and as such could not have caused it. Thus, without an external cause, i.e. God, the Big Bang is impossible.

The Koran, fourteen centuries before scientists discovered it, provided an accurate description of the Big Bang.

"Do not the unbelievers see that the skies and the earth were one unit (joined together), then we split them apart..." Koran 21:30

The Arabic word used in the Koran to signify separation in the above statement is *Fataq*. It means to disjoint or disunite. It essentially captures, in the description, "symmetry breaking" between particles and forces that modern cosmologists talk about in explaining the complexity of the Universe.

SOME CONCEPTS:

If it is said that the Universe is *open*, it means it will expand forever. If it is said that it is *closed*, it will not expand forever. Whether a Universe will expand, depends on its average density. If that density is less than or equal to its critical density, the Universe will expand. Our Universe at present according to estimates has less than 20% of the density of matter needed to stop it from expanding. Essentially, it will continue to expand.

The Universe is not "beginning-less". It was "born" out of the Big Bang and had a beginning. Some people maintain the unscientific idea that the Universe is "beginning-less" like the Steady-State theory advocated. Not only has that theory fallen out of favor due to the evidence, but also the *Second Law of Thermodynamics* contradicts the assertion that the Universe is "beginning-less". There is a well-acknowledged silent "rule" among scientists, which put into crude language states: *"In your research do not mess with the Second Law of Thermodynamics"*. In a closed system (by closed here I mean one which does not take energy from the outside—this is different to the closed definition given above), entropy, a measure of the degree to which a systems energy is unavailable to perform useful work, increases with time. To restate this: In a system, which does not take energy from the outside, like our Universe, entropy increases with time.

If the Universe had existed forever, we would see maximum entropy (complete disorder), which we do not see at all, something referred to as the *fate of excessive expansion*. This in short is why the *Second Law of Thermodynamics* does not agree with a beginning-less Universe.

THE DARK NIGHT SKY PARADOX:

If the Universe were infinite in spatial extent then light from infinite number of stars would always be pouring down on the earth from the skies. A simple mathematical calculation would show that the sky would never be dark under such circumstances. The paradox can only be resolved if we assume a *finite* age of the Universe (i.e. a beginning). In such a case, which corresponds to reality, we are only able to see the light, which has had time to travel across space to earth since the beginning of the particular star from which it comes (Davies 1982:46).

GOD & THE BIG BANG:

1. The Flatness Problem in Cosmology:

The actual density of the Universe is the average amount of matter or mass-energy per unit of space. If the actual density of the Universe is greater than a particular critical density then the Universe will eventually stop expanding. Since after more than 10 billion years of expanding, the Universes actual density is pretty close to its critical density, scientists conclude that at the time of the Big Bang, these two figures must have been very close to each other. They do not know why this was so. If it had not been so, and the actual density differed from the critical by even a tiny amount, either way, our Universe would have ceased to exist after only a few million years. This is termed as the *flatness* problem. They do not know why both the figures were where they were supposed to be, to make our Universe still exist after 10 billion years.

The Koran talked about the "expanding Universe" as well, fourteen centuries before scientists discovered it:

> "And the sky, we built it with might and We cause the <u>expansion of it</u>." Koran 51:47

If the Universe had been expanding too rapidly, the clouds that formed the galaxies would have been spread thin and pulled apart before gravity could dominate. On the other hand, if the Universe had started out expanding too slowly, it would have come to a halt and started to re-collapse with galaxies falling towards each other (Gribbins, Rees 17)

If we push back to the earliest time at which our theories of physics can be thought to have any validity, the implication is that the "density-parameter" was set in the beginning, with an accuracy of 1 part in 10^{60} (10 followed by 60 zeroes). Changing the parameter, either way, by a fraction given by a decimal point followed by sixty zeroes and a one; (0.00000000000000000000000000000000000000000000000000000000000001) would have made the Universe unsuitable for life, as we know it. (Gribbens, Rees 1989:18)

We are reminded of the "Flatness" of the Universe, its smoothness in this statement of the Koran:

> "[It is God] who has created the multiple skies, one separate from the other (as layers). You cannot see any flaw in the Merciful (God's) creation. Look again, can you make out any rifts?" (Koran 67:3)

<u>2. The Horizon or the Isotropy Problem:</u>

At around 300,000 years after the Big Bang, all parts of the Universe, even separated by more than 20 times the horizon distance, and expanding in opposite directions, in causally disconnected regions (i.e. no cause or physical effect could pass from one region to the other), began to expand with the same expansion rate and temperature.

No natural explanation exists to explain how a chaotic explosion, the Big Bang resulted in a uniform expansion pattern among causally disconnected regions, expanding in opposite directions. Calculations indicate that when the Universe was a trillionth of a trillionth of a trillionth second old, it consisted of 10 to the power 80 causally disconnected regions, and no physical effect could have traveled from one region to another and yet 300,000 years after, cosmic background radiation proves that they all started expanding with the same expansion rate and the same temperature.

The Koran informs us of the uniformity of cause in the early Universe:

> "...And He (God) inspired in all the heavens their mandate (Koran 41:12)."

HOW GALAXIES BECAME POSSIBLE:

Calculations by cosmologists indicate that matter in the early Universe was uniformly distributed and hence gravitational contractions (contraction is opposite of expansion) in an expanding Universe could not have taken place due to natural circumstances unless some special features were *built-in* into the system about one second after the Big Bang (by intelligence). This is exactly what the *inflation* explanation implies as well. If the Big Bang were a chance event what we would see would be a disorderly arrangement of matter with no galaxies and no order. An intelligent designer controlled things

> "...And we decked the skies of the world with lamps.... Such is the calculation of the Mighty (God), the Knower." Koran 41:12

Einstein's *General Theory of Relativity* leads scientists to conclude that in its earliest instant, the Universe was infinitely dense where its diameter was zero, i.e. nothing. Yes, the Universe was literally nothing at one time. God creates out of nothing. The Koran describes creation out of nothing as an attribute unique to God.

NATURAL AND SUFFICIENT REASONS FOR THE CONSTANTS?

There can be natural and sufficient reasons for some physical characteristics of the Universe but not all. Without suitable constants, life as we know it would not have existed and there would be no one to wonder about the cosmos.

Consider this analogy by a Canadian philosopher, John Leslie: Suppose you are facing execution by a fifty-man firing squad. The bullets are fired and you find that all have missed their target. Had they not done so you would not have survived to ponder the matter. But realizing that you are alive, you would legitimately be perplexed and wonder why (Gribbens, Rees 1989: 271).

1. *The law of conservation of mass and energy:* The mass-energy in the Universe neither increases nor decreases. Therefore the total amount of mass-energy in the Universe has been the same and will remain the same. If someone were to figure out the mass-energy total in the Universe and give it a figure say X, no natural explanation can exist on why it is X and not X+100 or X-100 and so on.

2. *The Constants:* There are no natural and sufficient reasons why all of the Universe's constants have the values they have. If they had different values, life would cease to exist. However they have the values they have regardless of any physical necessity. Examples like the Planck's constant, the speed of light, the electron charge, and the gravitational constant etc. These constants with the exception of the gravitational constant have not varied more than one percent since the start of the Universe. The gravitational constant has varied around ten percent.

It should be noted at this point that these constants have been there since the beginning of the Universe, a time before life appeared. These and other strange laws of nature defy any natural and sufficient reasons for their existence, the only valid explanation left is that an intelligent designer set them:

> "...The calculation of the Mighty (God), the Knower." Koran 41:12

According to the *principle of sufficient reason* stated by G.W. Leibniz, "No fact can be real or existing and no statement true unless there is a SUFFICIENT reason why anything is the way it is and not otherwise."

Whereas scientists face an enigma here, which threatens the edifice of their work, the followers of the Koran face no such enigma at all. God is the sufficient reason. The cause of the constants:

> "To Him submits whatsoever is in the heavens and the earth." (Koran)

SUITABLE CONSTANTS:

> "The numerical values that nature has assigned to the fundamental constants, such as the charge on the electron, the mass of the proton, and the Newtonian Gravitational constant, may be mysterious, but they are critically relevant to the structure of the Universe that we perceive. As more and more physical systems from nuclei to galaxies have become better understood, scientists have begun to realize that many characteristics of these systems are remarkably sensitive to the precise value of the fundamental constants. Had nature opted for a slightly different set of numbers, the world would have been a very different place and we would not be here to see it (Davies 1982)."

The quote by Paul Davies above summarizes the *Anthropic Principle* in cosmology, a premise the conclusion of which the Koran mentions in this statement:

> "Do you not see that God has utilized (or subjected or made subservient) for them whatsoever is in the heavens and on earth."(Koran 31:20)

All the constants in the heavens and earth have been subjected to make sure that life and humanity came to be. This is a fact given the current state of evidence. There is no natural explanation as to why the constants have the values they have. They have been set with a purpose in mind, with intelligence and *subjected* to make sure that the Universe evolved in the way that it did and life and humanity came to be.

i) <u>Proton Charge</u>: All protons in the Universe have a positive charge of 1.6×10 to the power-19 coulomb. This causes the various protons in the atoms to repel one another, but at the same time they stay together since the attraction is 100 times stronger than the repulsion.

Now the proton has a mass that is 1836 times that of an electron, yet for some mysterious reason the charge on the electron is the same as the proton, 1.6×10 to the power-19 coulomb. Suppose the proton had a lesser charge than what it actually does, there is no reason why it should not have, there is no natural explanation on why it does not, then the attraction between protons would be much more than we see with present figures and they would collide more. This, scientists say would lead to the stars using up their thermonuclear fuel in their cores much faster and dying out in about 100 million years. On our planet it took about 3 billion years for life to appear. If the lives of stars were 100 million years then life could exist nowhere on the Universe. An intelligent designer put the figures where they were supposed to be, at 1.6×10^{19}.

ii) <u>The Strong Force</u>: The neutrons and protons in the nucleus of the atoms are referred to as nucleons, since they exist in the nucleus. If the neutrons and the protons are separated by more than a hundred billionth of a centimeter, there is no mutual attraction between them. However when separated by a distance of less than ten trillionth of a centimeter, they feel a strong force of attraction. This is termed as a Strong Force or Strong Nuclear Force.

Scientists calculate that during the first few minutes after the expansion began, roughly 25% of the hydrogen in the Universe was converted to helium. Scientists also say that if the strong force had been any more

intense (which requires a shift in a trillionth of a centimeter or less), all of the Universe's hydrogen would have been converted to helium. In such a case life would never exist for 3 reasons:
1) There would be no water without hydrogen.
2) Hydrogen is necessary for proteins and nucleic acids that are needed for life.
3) Stars that have only helium are extremely short lived and could never reach the three billion years figure that our system took for life to appear.

What if the strong force were a little weaker by a trillionth of a centimeter or less, things just would not exist as the protons could not stay together in the cores of atoms. It is an acknowledged fact that if the Strong Force was not between 0.1 f and 2 f (where f is the Strong Force constant) life would not exist and nor would any order as we see it. The difference between the two figures is less than microscopic and there is no explanation on why the numbers were where they were. Just this one constant happening by chance, is by itself, other things being equal, one in one million. When you take into account all the other constants, the figure gets so small that to believe that life originated without an intelligent designer becomes more absurd than the most absurd fairy tale imaginable.

The law of conservation of mass and energy discussed earlier makes it impossible to attribute a "natural" cause to the start of the Universe. The energy had to come from somewhere, the energy whose radiation we still receive.

At Planck time (which is 10 to the power of negative 43 seconds, i.e. 10^{-43}) which was a microscopic fraction of the first second after the Universe began to expand, all the matter that we observe in the Universe was less than a tenth of a millimeter across in volume. According to the theory of black holes, the gravity of this singularity would be so massive that apart from a faint type of quantum radiation nothing at all could escape from it.

Astronomers know that no natural cause could have caused the explosion of energy given the gravity of the singularity. No known natural force could have overcome even a tenth of the gravity of the singularity at the time of the Big Bang.

"...*And We split them apart.*" *(Koran 21:30).*

Consider this principle in science:

<u>Occam's Razor:</u>

"*When giving explanations, it is better to give a simpler explanation that assumes the existence of fewer unproved things.*"

Apart from providing greater credibility to what we've established above this idea throws more light on:

1. Why there is just one God and not "gods" given the organization and the uniformity in the Universe. The fundamental postulate of Einstein's *Special Theory of Relativity* states this unity of law phenomena in nature.

"*If there were in them (the heavens and the earth) other gods beside GOD, there would have been confusion in both.*" *(Koran 21:22)*

2. If there were more than one God then different parts of the Universe would not have worked with such uniformity as they did and as has always been the case. Also, parts of the matter in the Universe would have originated at different times. Yet scientists agree that the Big Bang was when all energy and matter originated in the Universe.

"*There has never been any other god besides God. Otherwise, each god would have declared independence with their creations, and they would have competed with each other for dominance. GOD be glorified; far above their claims.*" *(Koran 23:91)*

<u>WHO CREATED GOD?</u>

After exhausting all the other alternatives, the only hypothesis that is logically deduced from empirical evidence provided by nature, is that an intelligent being created the heavens and the earth. This being cannot be "human" or like anything in the natural world, so to speak. The attributes of the Universe that "necessitate" design (discussed above) as well as the attributes in us that "necessitate" design (discussed below) cannot be the attributes of a creator otherwise "it" would need a creator as well. Thus, if the creator is "different" than creation, in the attributes that "it" possesses, the question "Who created God?" becomes logically meaningless. Intelligent design would apply only to things that were non-existent and then came into being and contain specific attributes that necessitate design. Thus God has to be eternal, unchanging and unlike creation.

"Say: He is Allah (the God) the One. God, the eternal, absolute. He begets not, nor was He begotten and there is none like Him." (Koran 112)

THE PLANCK CONSTANT:

The Planck Constant is fixed at 6.6 X (10 to the power of-23) erg per second. It is a figure that shows up in all major equations used by nuclear physicists. The energy used by anything is always some multiple of Planck's Constant. There is no natural reason why the Planck's Constant is where it is, it could be a lot higher or a lot lower, but it has been balanced at this level without any natural reason.

The PC (Planck's Constant) appears in an important formula used to determine the "Fine structure Constant." The formula is e^2/hc where "e" is the electron charge, "h" is the PC and "c" is the speed of light.

If the Planck's constant had been greater by just 0.00000001, all the stars in our system would be red. If it was lower by just 0.00000001 all the stars in our system would be blue. The problem with red stars is that they never erupt as supernova and if there are no supernovas there are no higher-level elements that are necessary for life. If there were no supernova, there would be no carbon to start carbon-based life like us. Blue stars on the other hand burn only for a short time, i.e. around 150 million years. However, it took nearly 3 billion years or more for life to emerge on earth. One hundred and fifty million just would just not cut it. The designer, to make sure that life emerged, set this constant.

THE SPEED OF LIGHT:

The speed of light is set at $3 \times (10^8)$ meters per second. It is an important constant which figures in Einstein's famous formula $E=mc^2$. "E" is the energy produced when matter is converted to energy in thermonuclear reactions in stars. If the speed of light had been just a tiny fraction higher (and there is no natural reason why it is not) then thermonuclear reactions would produce over 10,000 times more energy and all the fuel in the star core would be used up much quicker. Stars would die out much sooner than the 3 billion years it took for life to emerge on earth. Hence life would never have happened.

On the other hand if it were just a little tiny fraction lower, the early Universe expansion would have been much slower and long ago the Universe would have suffered a gravitational collapse. So both ways there would be no life. An intelligent designer who had planned the emergence of life set this constant.

NEUTRON MASS:

Neutrons have a constant mass of 1.67×10^{-24} grams. When outside an atom a neutron is very unstable and quickly decays into a proton and electron. Inside the nucleus it is stable and does not decay. Suppose that the mass of the neutron was 2% greater than what it is now (and why should it not have been?) neutrons would rapidly decay and an atom would become unstable. As a fact, no higher elements would exist which are necessary for life. The only element in the entire Universe would be hydrogen.

On the other hand, if the neutron had a mass less than its current mass by a tiny fraction, the protons would become unstable. This is because now the protons would have a higher mass than neutrons in the nucleus and they would decay into neutrons or positive positrons or pions. According to physicists, if the neutron mass were 0.998 of its present mass, the decay of protons would make the existence of atoms impossible. There would be no life. The designer had life in mind when He set the balance.

"...*He (God) has set the balance.*" Koran 55:7

Donald Page of the Princeton Institute of Advanced Study has calculated the odds against the formation of our Universe without God putting in the necessary constants. And the figure comes out to be one out of 10,000,000,000 to the power 124. To see how impossible it is compare this number to the total amount of subatomic particles in the whole Universe, which has been calculated to be 10 to the power 80.

Beginning-less is illogical, philosophically speaking:

If the Universe was not created then it must have existed for an infinite time in the past. However, us being in the present make such a statement preposterous. It is not possible to cross an actual infinity. No matter how much you count or how much time passes, there would still be more to count or more time to pass. This is what the definition of actual infinity is. It is nonfinite; it has no room for growth. If the past were infinite, then to get to the present moment, we would have had to cross an actual infinite. In the language of math and logic this is gibberish. It is just like saying that you can jump out of a bottomless pit. This concept throws light on the attributes of God, the creator also. The one who started this, himself must have had to be logically speaking, timeless and unchanging. This also tells us that, since the Universe had a beginning, God is not the same as the Universe (which is a popular view) and God is not contained in the Universe (also a popular view), as at one time the Universe was a singularity.

The Odds:

Roger Penrose, one of the worlds leading physicists, in his book, *The Emperor's New Mind* (1989) states:

> "This now tells us how precise the Creator's aim must have been, namely to an accuracy of $(10^{10})^{123}$. This is an extraordinary figure. One could not even possibly write the number down in the ordinary notation: it would be one followed by 10^{123} successive 0's. Even if we were to write a zero on each separate proton and each separate neutron in the entire Universe—and we could throw in all the other particles for good measure—we should fall far short of writing the figure needed" (as quoted by Denton 1998:9).

The Koran informed us of this, centuries earlier:

> "If you were to <u>count</u> the blessings of God towards you, you can never put a number on them (14:34)"

The Reality of the Universe:

> "…Whenever He (God) decrees a matter, He says "Be" and it is. (Koran)."

According to the "Copenhagen" approach to quantum systems (based upon which the singularity of the Big Bang is studied by cosmologists, because Classical physics breaks down at the quantum level), objects are "real" ONLY when an act of observation by an observer "collapses the wave function" granting the system into one or the other of its potential states (Ferris, Timothy 1997:255). The "wave function" of the Universe could never have collapsed without the "observation" of an observer, i.e. God. The Koran states:

> "To God is due the <u>starting point</u> (primal origin, Badeeh in Arabic) of the skies and the earth. And Whenever He (God) decrees a matter, He says to it, "Be" and it is."(Koran 2:117).

Timothy Ferris states in his book, <u>The Whole Shebang</u>:
> "...The Copenhagen interpretation of quantum mechanics treats as real only observed phenomena, raising the riddle how the EARLY Universe could have evolved in the absence of observers. The riddle may be "solved" by invoking God as the supreme observer, who by scrutinizing all particles converts their quantum potentials into actual states." (Ferris, page 308)

DNA: Mark of the Creator:

> "Which is it, of the benefits of your Cherisher (God), that you deny?"
> (Koran 55:Multiple)

Some atheist scientists who were unaware of the wonderful program, the complex mechanism of RNA and DNA were of the *outmoded* opinion that due to favorable physical influences, chemical compounds were able to spontaneously combine in an organized fashion and hence, were by magic, able to produce the fantastic complex which we call a cell, and then even more fantastic complexes like rudimentary living organism.

Given that all their intelligence and directed efforts to date have been unable to form one single living cell in the laboratory, shows that the problems with spontaneous generation of life from chemicals are enormous. Indeed for the smallest macromolecules of a cell to form as a result of repeated attempts, such enormous quantities of matter would have been processed that they would have filled colossal masses on the scale comparable to the volume of the earth itself. Contrary to this we see beauty and harmony in nature and variety of all created things. Chance is totally inconceivable (Bucaille 1987).

Oparine, a modern Russian biologist, who is a well-known materialist, rejects outright the theory of chance in the formation of life. An article,"*The current state of the problem of the origin of life and its future perspectives*", states from him:

> "The entire network of perpetual preservation and reproduction of the totality of conditions set by the external environment. This highly organized orientation characteristic of life cannot be the result of chance." (as quoted by Bucaille 1987)

The claims atheists make about a "chance" origin of life is tantamount to saying:

> "Iron ore and coal at high temperatures spontaneously formed steel particles and then those steel articles without any intelligence involved(by magic) formed the Eiffel Tower and other structures (Bucaille 1987)."

This statement sounds ignorant in the context of a man-made steel structure, but saying that a cell formed by itself is even more atrocious because a cell is much more complex than any steel structure that human intelligence (not chance) has built.

In his book, *The Origin of Life,* Oparine draws particularly relevant comparisons to convince the layman of the illogical nature of theories pointing towards chance. In 1954, he wrote:

> "It is as if one jumbled together the printing blocks representing the twenty-eight letters of the alphabet, in hope that by CHANCE, they will fall into a pattern of a poem that we know. Only through knowledge and careful arrangement of the letters and words in the poem however, can we produce the poem from the letters (page 52)."

The French surgeon, Maurice Bucaille correctly observes that each cell in the human body has a "program" analogous to a computer program written down, so well organized and regulated so as to function properly, the slightest malfunction leads to deformities and monstrous growths (cancer being the case in point). Each cell functions like a computer programmed to perform specific functions. It is common knowledge that a computer will only function if it has been programmed. A fact that implies the existence of a programming intellect that provides the information necessary to operate the system. The programming intellect for the billions of living cells, unvarying and uniform in his essence of programming is the One God.

The Hardware and the Software:

"He (Moses) said (to pharaoh), "Our Lord is He who gave to everything its creation, moreover guided it." Koran 20:5

There is a genuine enigma among the community of biologists, the origin of the genetic code and how it increases in information, which leads to more and more complex structures. The only valid explanation, given the intelligent nature of the messages contained in the DNA, is that an intelligent designer was involved. We call him Allah, the God.

The Enigma of Life's Origin:

The break between the living and non-living is the most fundamental of all discontinuities seen in nature. *Natural Selection* fails to explain this discontinuity, just as it failed to explain the discontinuity between species which biochemistry made clear.

Stanley Miller in the 1960s, in his attempt to simulate creation of life in the early earth, failed many times in his *"intelligently designed"* experiments before he succeeded in obtaining some amino acids, the building blocks of proteins. However, we are deliberately not told that he manipulated various scenarios of the early earth and not just one. We are also not told, in popular science textbooks, that he failed many times before he succeeded in his manipulations. His experiments were intelligently designed and not random chance, which make this entire effort worthless as it belies the basic premise of life evolving without intelligence. To form proteins from amino acids is a bigger problem than forming amino acids. However, our professors do not encourage us to think that no trial and error experiments were going on in the early earth using chemical beakers and flasks. Do we ever stop and think that _intelligent_ experiments are being designed and used by these "scientists" to deny that there was any _intelligence_ involved in the origin of life?

The "soup-theory" mentioned briefly above is the most in vogue among all the theories of the origin of life in the scientific community. However, it poses many questions and big problems and hence just like the pre-Miller times, it still remains an enigma. The "dawn-rocks" of Western Greenland, the earliest dated rocks on earth, considered to be about 3900 Million years old (dating from about 400 million years after the formation of the earth) do not show any trace of abiotically produced organic compounds. Sediments from various parts of the earth dated between 3900 and 3500 million years old also show no signs of any abiotically produced organic compounds. Like is the usual case with evolutionary theory by Natural Selection, paleontology does not support it.

In the Presence of oxygen, any organic compounds formed on the early earth would be rapidly oxidized and degraded. It is for this reason that advocates of the "soup" theory suggest (without any geo-chemical evidence to support what they are conjecturing) an early earth without oxygen. Only such an atmosphere would protect the compounds, which would then collect as the "soup". However this poses further problems. Without oxygen, there is no ozone layer in the upper atmosphere, which protects the earth from a lethal dose of ultraviolet radiation. In such a scenario, any organic compounds formed would break down in an instant. The empirical absence of organic compounds in Martian soil proves this. The late Carl Sagan recognized this when he stated that in the absence of oxygen, a lethal dose of ultraviolet radiation would reach the earth in 0.3 seconds.

The presence of water inhibits amino acids from joining to form proteins, since amino acids dissolve readily in water. To overcome this however, our ingenious atheist "scientists" have tried to "invent" another scenario. Sidney Fox says that the amino acids got washed to a hot pan-like land. However, experiments have shown that heating amino acids gives no proteins but a dark tar. However, they did some other manipulations by mixing and matching one part of three different amino acids to a beaker of purified amino acids they managed some joining among them. However, that did not yield any proteins but a chemically different product, which is now called proteinoid. The scientific community has thrown this theory out the door. One of the strongest critics of this theory was Stanley Miller.

Hoyle and his colleague Wickramasinge calculated the odds of the random formation of a single enzyme from amino acids anywhere on the early earth's surface as being 1 in 10^{20} (add 20 zeros after 1). To appreciate how impossible it is to get one enzyme anywhere on this earth from amino acids given the soup. But wait, there are not only one but two thousand enzymes, so the chance of obtaining all of these randomly would be 1 in $(10^{20})^{2000}$. This number for the odds is so small that it can hardly be distinguished from zero. It could never have happened even if the whole Universe was soup.

Biochemical systems, like blood clotting, vision, and many functions of the cell are *irreducibly complex*. Many systems backed by proper enzymes triggered by catalysts work together, automated to precision, working towards one desired goal in synchrony, to generate the result needed. No gradual system, like Natural Selection, can ever explain their origin. If one part is missing, the whole system fails. If one part is crude the consequences are disastrous. If we scan the literature that seeks to explain the development of these systems based on evolution by Natural Selection, there is none. Darwinism at the macro level requires faith, as there are *no scientific facts* to support it (Behe 1996).

Perverted Standards:

The human eye cannot see x-rays, electricity, magnetic fields etc, yet no man of science would dispute with their existence based on fact and proof. Yet, with just as much or more proof on God being the creator, the same scientists make the excuse, "We cannot see him." If today we were to receive even one intelligent message from space, scientists as a whole after confirmation would conclude that "yes, intelligent life in

5 / The Unifying Theory of Everything

has been confirmed." Yet, when millions of intelligent messages found in our DNA, the same scientists do not even look at it in consideration of an intelligent creator. Dogmatic scientists today have perverted standards.

An example of these perverted standards are theories like the "multiple Universe" theory. It is stated [as an escape from reality and the enigmas scientists face when they seek naturalistic explanations] that an infinite number of Universes exist; however we only see ours. The rest do exist somewhere else and all the possible combinations of constants are tried [by chance] and we were the lucky mix, so we are alive to ponder the Universe. What they do not realize is that in order to escape from the conclusion of one intelligent designer they are evoking infinite invisible Universes that can never be verified. *Occam's Razor* makes all this conjecture scientifically worthless. By abandoning *Occam's Razor*, some "scientists" are thus presenting to the world pseudo-science and dogmatism as pure science. It is not pure science rather it is pure dishonesty.

Not only is such an escape unscientific in its violation of "Occam's Razor" and that the entities evoked can never be scientifically verified, it runs into absurdities because it has to evoke the other fictitious "Universes" to the infinity because of the numbers above, which makes the whole argument collapse, logically speaking.

Martin Rees, a colleague of Stephen Hawking and one of the leading cosmologists in the world, writes:

> *Scientists commonly pay obeisance to "Ockham's razor"—the celebrated injunction by William of Ockham, in the early fourteenth century…Nothing perhaps could violate this more drastically than postulating an infinite array of Universes! Nor does it at first sight seem properly "scientific" to invoke regions that are unobservable and perhaps always will be (Rees 1997:247)*

The fact is that the world owes its being to something other than itself. The laws of nature did not create the Universe since they cease to exist at the earliest point in creation. The laws of mechanics did not originate the laws of mechanics because when the Universe was a singularity, they did not exist. The laws of evolution do not come about through the laws of evolution because in order to work they require a preexisting order and preexisting entities governed by that order.

According to Stephen Hawkings:
> But there is a problem with cosmology, because it cannot predict anything about the Universe without an assumption about the <u>initial conditions</u>...(as quoted by Zarata and McEvoy 1995:156).

Note:

The article above <u>does not</u> support in any way the Christian Creationists' position on humankind's origin. The Koran does not set a history of 6000 years for the world; neither does it support the unscientific ideas in the Bible.

Bibliography:

1. Mahin, Mark, <u>The New Scientific Case for God's Existence</u>. Mind lifter Press. 1985
2. Bucaille, Maurice, <u>What is the Origin of Man</u>. Seghers, Paris. (Reproduced by permission of the author). 1987
3. <u>Koran</u>: Translation from the Arabic.
4. Fred Hoyle And N. C Wickramasinge. <u>Evolution from Space</u>. Simon & Schuster 1981. NYC.
5. Dietrick E. Thomsen, <u>The Quantum Universe: A zero point fluctuation</u>.
6. Science News (3 August 1985), page, 73.
7. J.P Moreland, Kei Nielsen. <u>Does God Exist?</u> Prometheus Books. NY 1990.
8. Gribbins, John and Rees, Martin: <u>Cosmic Coincidences</u>. Bantam Books 1989.
9. Behe, Michael J. <u>Darwin's Black Box</u>. The Free Press 1996.

10. Davies, Paul. *The Accidental Universe*. Cambridge University Press, 1982.
11. Denton, Michael J. *Nature's Destiny*. 1998. New York: The Free Press.
12. Rees, Martin. 1997. *Before the Beginning*. Reading, Ma. Promethius Books.
13. Hawking, Stephen. 1998. *A Brief History of Time*. Bantam Books.
14. Zarata, Oscar and McEvoy, J.P. 1995. *Introducing Stephen Hawking*. Totem Books, New York.

EVOLUTION BY NATURAL SELECTION: ESTABLISHMENT CULTURE OR SCIENTIFIC FACT?

> *"Say: <u>travel in the earth</u> and see how God [Allah] originated creation…"*
> *(Koran 29:20)*

Charles Darwin was a graduate of Christ College in Cambridge. He was a clergyman with no previous background in biology or medicine. On December 21, 1831, Darwin sailed from Plymouth, England on the Beagle. His traveling in the earth to discover the origin of species was originally planned for two years but lasted five.

This voyage transformed the cleric into an independent and adventurous scientist who then proposed and embraced the idea of transmutation of species. Darwin's approach to discover the origin of species was a start in the right direction, but the pseudoscientific theory that he constructed based on it, has proved to be a leap backwards in what was to follow in origin biology.

<u>To date:</u>

1) No unequivocal scientific evidence exists in favor of evolution by Natural Selection changing specie types on a grand scale.

2) Darwin himself in his letters confessed that his theory cannot be demonstrated scientifically in any case [i.e. one species evolving into another] but it helps explain a lot of things [even the explanations he sought in the light of modern discovery are faulty especially concerning rudimentary organs].

Evolution is a pseudoscientific and not a scientific theory according to the very definition of a scientific theory. According to the *Oxford Dictionary*, for a theory to be classified as scientific, it must embody in itself <u>facts</u> within a framework of general laws.

The History:

In the 6th Century BC, Anaximander of Miletus introduced the notion of evolution in the animal kingdom. In the century after, Lucretius, in his book, "On Nature," seemed to favor a notion of Natural Selection that preserves the strongest species. Buffon (1707-1788) supported evolution but being afraid of challenging the established ideas of the day retracted. Lamarck in 1801, before Darwin, outlined his theory of evolution in his book, "Zoological Philosophy [La Philosophie zoologique]." (Bucaille 1987)

Lamarck theorized that the environment has a tremendous influence on living organisms as a result of which they change to adapt. The change he said is hereditary and is passed on to the next generation. The change would be of growing complexity when it was favorable and when an organ was not used it would atrophy (Bucaille 1987).

Lamarck was incorrect in his theorizing about the hereditary nature of newly acquired characteristics, however, his ideas provided Darwin with something to work with. Thus, Lamarck and not Darwin is the actual "Father of Natural [materialistic] Evolution." Darwin was also influenced by Malthus and bought into the theory of geometric increase in population. He makes mention of it in the introduction to the second edition (1860) of, *On the Origin of Species* (Bucaille 1987).

Biologists long before Darwin grouped animals together according to some similarity and relationship. Taxonomists, for example, before Darwin classified whales and bats as mammals and not fish and bird because in "essence" they had features of mammals. The difference between pre-Darwinian taxonomists and Darwin was that they attributed the similarity to a "blue print" existing with God and Darwin attributed it to a natural gradual change from one to the other. Thus Darwin's theory explained (without empirical evidence) the similar structures employed for classification i.e. homology (Johnson 1993).

Evolution by Natural Selection happens in slow steps?

A slow mechanism of evolution as envisioned by the theory of Evolution by Natural Selection necessitates innumerable transitional forms. Darwin acknowledged this:

> *That Natural Selection generally acts with extreme slowness, I duly admit…. As Natural Selection acts solely by accumulating slight, successive, favorable variations, it can produce no <u>great or sudden modifications</u>; it can act only by short and slow steps (Darwin: On the Origin of Species).*

When objections arose as to why we do not find the intermediary forms in fossil records, the only answer Darwin and his supporters could give was that they are present but have not been dug up yet. While it might have carried some weight in his day but today with so much paleontological excavations, whenever a new find is unearthed it belongs to a well-developed isolated class or a class we are already well aware of, and cannot even one instance be classified as an intermediary.

The isolation of classes in all of paleontology and in the observable natural world are absolute and transitions to particular characteristic traits are abrupt and the phenomena of discontinuity is universal throughout the living kingdom. Darwin's theory of Evolution failed in its attempt to predict reality.

Darwin's theory cannot be termed a scientific fact. It deals with unique events, i.e. the origin of life, the origin of intelligence, the origin of higher species etc. Unique events like the ones evolutionary theory deals with are unrepeatable and therefore can never be subject to scientific experimentation.

However when theories like evolution become the "in-thing" in society, they are given a very high "status" and it is expected that people accept them just at "face-value" even though empirical proof has never been presented or substantiated. The theory as such becomes a cultural dogma, an ideological norm of the scientific establishment (the ruling paradigm). Questioning such a theory becomes akin to apostasy and is met with hate and emotion rather than scientific evidence. Consider for example the faith that Dawkins, the author of *The Blind Watchmaker*, has in Darwin's "church":

> "The theory (of evolution) is about as much in doubt as the earth goes around the sun."(*The Selfish Gene*, page 1, 1976)
> This is an atrocious claim. Darwin acknowledged that empirical evidence did not exist in support of his theory whereas empirical evidence exists in support of the earth going around the sun.

Richard Dawkins, the author of *The Blind Watchmaker*, by playing with his 64Kb computer (a dinosaur that has long been extinct as far as computers go), envisions proving evolution. It is amazing to note his ideas about "biomorphs" producing figures, which to his mind resembled insects and bats (out of a million zillion garbage figures). I can find a bat or an insect in a blot of ink too if I look close enough. Do you know about the Rosach Ink blot test? I can even see a man in a patch of ink. The imagination fills in the gaps. The only thing the whole discussion on "biomorphs" proves is a vivid imagination and a force fitting of it to a theory.

Dawkins also overlooked, rather conveniently, the fact that any program involves the existence of a programming intellect that provides the information necessary to operate the system. The laws of evolution could not have originated the laws of evolution since even according to the theory they require a specific order and entities governed by that order.

Evolutionists and Neo-Darwinians classify cells as evolved. This is not true: Ninety nine percent of cellular structures all across the species are identical. This figure is 100% for DNA. The only difference between cells is the "program" which instructs them on how to function. Darwinists have not shown to date how the cell with its irreducibly complex features could have evolved through successive corrections. Thus evolutionary theory fails at the basic cell level.

Every cell is programmed to function in a specific way. Even the ordinary computer user knows that a computer, with all its complex structures [hardware], will only function if it has been programmed. A fact that implies the existence of a programming intellect that provides the information required [software] to operate the system. This should surely lead one to consider the role of the Creator in life's existence.

> "He [Moses] said [to Pharaoh]: `Our Cherisher (God) is He who gave to everything its creation then guided it." Koran 20:5

There is a genuine enigma, an ignorance faced by the medical and biological community throughout the world: the origin of the genetic code. It has not been demonstrated yet how the "increase in data," contained in the genes leads to complex structures.

> "Say: `Is there any of your associates [whom you hold equal to God], one who produces creation then reproduces it?' Say: `Allah (God) produces creation then reproduces it. How, then are you mislead." (Koran 10:34)

The one who originated the genetic code has the power to reproduce it, to add to it or take away from it, which can be defined as *Directed Evolution*, and not blind Natural Selection. Whereas "Microevolution" is seen to operate in nature and which Darwin documented in his voyage on the Beagle, it operates within the same species. For example the variation in Finches that Darwin documented as well as the darkening of the color of the wing of the moth after the industrial revolution (because of pollution) so that it can better escape predators are examples of microevolution. However, this small scale cannot be applied to the whole class of living organisms with the conclusion that everything in nature happened by happy coincidences and survival correction with no intelligence involved. There is complete lack of empirical evidence to support the notion that Macroevolution works in nature based solely on Natural Selection. There is no evidence whatsoever which can prove that Natural Selection has transformed one species into another on the "grand scale" (bigger than the intelligently directed separation of fruit flies, which nature didn't change but human intelligence did) of the natural world.

The flaw in Darwin's conjecture was that he translated evolution working within species without empirical evidence, into the concept of his *General Theory of Evolution* by which he sought to explain the origin of life on this planet. The mechanism operating within birds, to change their beak sizes for example or the color of the wing of the moth, are minute and microscopic compared to a change, say in a cell to form a human brain. Natural Selection could never have achieved that even by a wild swing of the imagination. In a letter to Asa Grey, which Darwin wrote on September 5, 1857, he says,

"Ones imagination must FILL UP the very wide blanks."

Another thing that Darwin overlooked, being really impressed with the new theory in Geology, of gradual change in the surface of the earth, was that *Micro* changes do not always translate into *Macro* changes. For example, the day to day weather changes that we experience are caused by different reasons than the Macro changes in climate, caused by the earth's journey around the sun. Also consider Geology, the Micro changes caused by weathering, sedimentary deposition, volcanic activity are different to the Macro changes caused by Plate Tectonics.

Consider an argument from language: In order to change this simple word "SAT" into a fairly simple sentence, "HE**SAT**ON THE MAT," we need an addition to information which is not contained in the word SAT. Natural Selection cannot explain the origin of the new information. The origin of the genetic code and how it increases in information is an enigma to all biologists, Darwinian or non-Darwinian. There are many modern biologists who do not accept Darwin's ideas but there are no modern physicists who do not buy into the fact that the earth goes around the sun.

Explaining the addition to the information needed to transform a simple word to a very simple sentence cannot be explained by Natural Selection. Even to change the sentence: "He sat on the mat," to "He stood on the mat," we would need not a step by step change but a simultaneous change to keep the sentence stable given the criteria of English.

Step by Step Change:
He**SAT**on the mat
He**ST**on the mat
He**STO**on the mat
He*STOO**on the mat
He*STOOD**on the mat

Now count the transitory unstable "species" in the transformation. They come to a minimum of 3. Note also that sentence 2-4 are non-functional compared to sentence 1 and 5. According to the very definition of Natural Selection, which is supposed to preserve beneficial changes, the transitory forms do not work. Further in all the excavations of paleontology there is no shred of evidence of numerous intermediary forms, the number of which should be millions of times more than stable species, according to the theory.

The facts support a simultaneous and coordinated change, the addition in information coming from an "intelligent" source, the originator of the genetic code. As an example consider the evolution of the horse which took place on different continents under different conditions which would have yielded different results according to Natural Selection and not the uniform result we see.

Consider what the natural world shows:

Biologists today know that every organized being forms as a whole, by itself a unique and perfect system, the parts of which correspond and function mutually. None of the parts can change one at a time as Natural Selection predicts without the whole changing or there is no harmony, the kind of harmony we see in nature. The isolation and distinctiveness of species and the existence of clear discontinuities in nature are self-evident. Paleontology does not find any evidence of innumerable intermediaries between species leading up to the perfectly adapted final. All they find is thousands of identical individuals that are distinct and isolated and functionally adapted and cannot be termed as intermediaries. Natural data supports the notion of gaps and jumps in the organization and complexity of species, and not unstable intermediaries.

The fossil record in the natural world consistently shows two things. Johnson quotes Harvard Professor Stephen J. Gould, a well-known evolutionist, when he explains this:

1. *Stasis: Most species exhibit no directional change during their tenure on earth. They appear in fossil record looking pretty much the same as when they disappear; morphological change is usually limited [like in Microevolution] and directionless.*
2. *Sudden appearance [as against the gradual improvement and appearance]. In any local area, a species does not arise gradually by the steady transformation of its ancestors; it appears all at once and "fully formed"* (As cited in Johnson 1993:50).

Both these facts, well documented, contradict evolution by Natural Selection. What keeps Darwinism alive and well in the hearts of modern day scientists is what keeps Christianity alive in the hearts of Christians, i.e. faith. There is no empirical evidence, and no verification by scientific facts to back the theory.

Neo-Darwinians sometimes cite the example of the Lung Fish, which has the gill structure of the fish but a heart of an amphibian, as an intermediary. This however is incorrect because of two reasons: 1) Their theory does not point to just one but millions of intermediaries. So there is not only one missing link but zillions of missing links 2) The lung fish cannot be termed as an intermediary because it is a perfect system: the gills/respiration works like a perfect fish and the heart like a perfect amphibian. There is no unstable intermediary "thing" in the lungfish which Natural Selection will correct via its zillions more intermediary stages. Neither do the gills show anything that is a transition between the fish and an amphibian.

Concerning the fish story, P.P Grasse, the eminent French Zoologist states:

> *"What makes us particularly unwilling to accept the story of the little fish—the 'Magellan of evolution'—is the fact that the boleophthalmidae and periophthalmidae (mud skippers) perform this very experiment [of trying to explore dry land, as the Darwinian story goes]. They scuttle across the mud, climb the roots of mangrove trees, and raise themselves on their pectoral fins, just as if the limbs were short limbs. They have lived in this way for millions of years, and although they never stop leaping about—awkwardly or not—their fins insist on remaining as they are, rather than transforming themselves into limbs. These animals are not really very understanding [of Darwin]."* (As quoted by Bucaille 1987: 56).

Consider the fact that nature's distinctions are clear. The group-type mammals for example, the Kangaroo, the mouse and the man all have the basic mammalian characteristics of hair and mammary glands and due to these and other common features stand distinct from other vertebrate (those having back bones) species. If Macroevolution were the case and a fact like Dawkins states then nature's divisions would not be so distinct but blurred just as evolutionary theory predicts. This is exactly what we do not find in nature or the fossil record.

How do you explain "Panchronic" species?

If Natural Selection was a fact, just like the earth going around the sun, as Dawkins claims, then how can you explain certain species, which have failed to evolve at all even though they undergo mutations like all other species? The Panchronic species stand as a challenge to Neo-Darwinism.

As examples:

1. Bees from the tertiary period are the same as today's bees. Consider the bee's sting, which ensures its death (not survival). If Natural Selection was the law, why did not the bee sting evolve into something that did ensure survival and not death?

2. The coelacanth, caused great excitement when it was first discovered. It dates from the Cretaceous period, 130 million years back. They were thought to be extinct but one live specimen was discovered in 1938, which is the same as its ancestors. When it was dissected, its internal organs showed no sign of being pre-adapted to a land environment and gave no clue as to how it could develop into an amphibian (Johnson 1993: 76)

3. In plants, there is a living plant fossil known as gingko that has leaves unlike that of any modern tree.

4. The Lampreys are jaw-less fishes. If developing jaws was such a big advantage according to evolutionary theory, how come these jaw-less, lower stage fishes do so well? How come the intermediary stage between jaw-less and jawed fish died out (with no fossil evidence) but the original primitive jaw-less fish survived?

5. Bacteria although they reproduce and hence mutate faster should have evolved more if Natural Selection was the case. However fossil bacteria going back to 3.5 billion years are identical with today's modern forms.

6. Blue Algae, have been in existence for over one billion years, and are the same as today's algae. Also the opossum, which has been around for millions of years without evolving. Sponges and cockroaches are also good examples.

7. Fish lacking vision and also fish possessing sonar [sonic radar] systems and fish that "see" by electric fields live side by side at the bottom of the ocean. If evolutionist were correct then the blindfish should have been replaced long time ago by the other two yet they have survived side by side for millions of years.

> "And how many an animal there is that bears not its own provision! Allah [God] provides for it and for you. He is the Hearer, the Knower." Koran 29:60

Biologists state that evolution in fishes and humans has come to a stand still. If we seek an answer of "why?" from Darwin's theory, we fail to find one.

Excessive Evolution:

If Natural Selection was a fact, then how come certain animals show excessive "evolutionary" development, if you accept the premise of evolutionary theory that calls for better adaptation? For example:

i) The Irish elk with its excessive antlers which causes a hindrance rather than an advantage to the animal in question. Evolutionists say that the development of antlers was an "chance" benefit of Natural Selection. Why didn't Natural Selection correct it and prevent it from being excessive in the case of the Irish elk?

ii) There are Mollusks living on coral reefs the shells of, which have become so over-thickened that they can hardly open them to feed.

It seems like in their case as in the many other cases that Natural Selection "died" as a natural law. However, the law that makes the earth go around the sun is uniform in all regions of the Universe as regards bodies which move relative to each other. So much for Dawkins' physics.

Lack of Features?

Whereas the evolutionists are fast to explain why certain features appear in species, they never explain the lack of those features or why they do not appear in some. As examples, consider the cilia (motile hairs) which are absent in spiders and eel worms while they occur in a wide range of other creatures ranging from protozoan to man. Why are pigmented cells, which affect color changes to protect certain animals, absent from all warm-blooded animals. They would indeed be of as much advantage to them as to cold-blooded animals?

Variety:

If Natural Selection were the blind case then everything would have developed in one direction only. Just look at even the sizes of everything: Lizards—big like crocodiles and small; cats small and big like the lion; pigs, the guinea pig and the wild boar. Indeed the variety within species that does not serve any adaptive advantage has always proved challenging for evolutionists to explain away.

"And of His [God's] signs is the creation of the skies and the earth and all the variety of beasts that he has dispersed in them. And He is able to gather them whenever He wills." Koran 42:29

Variety suggests intelligently directed change:

"That so many diverse forms of life and basically dissimilar body plans have in fact been actualized during the course of evolution on earth, supports the concept that the evolutionary tree of life on earth was generated from a unique PROGRAM embedded in the order of nature, and that was specifically arranged to generate through a myriad of unique and intricate transformations, the fullest possible plentitude of natural biological forms." (Denton 1998:320)

Indeed, We created you according to the best organizational plan (taqweem) Koran 95:4

Artificial Selection is not the same as Natural Selection:

Darwin linked Natural Selection to artificial selection practiced by man, in influencing certain characteristics in farm or other animals [selective breeding]. Modern Neo-Darwinists use the same analogy. However there are serious flaws in this analogy [as cited in Bucaille (1987) and Johnson (1993)]:

i) Artificial selection does not create new species, as is claimed for Natural Selection.
ii) Artificial selection does not create new functional organs or a new organization or a new genus, as Natural Selection is supposed to in the "minds" of the Darwinists
iii) Artificial Selection does not work using "blind" nature and chance but intelligence.
iv) When animals altered by artificial selection are returned to the natural environment the "highly specialized breeds" die out and not the "weaker" ones that occur in nature.

Natural Selection, which implies "Survival of the Fittest", is a circular argument that applies a tautology [a way of saying the same thing twice]. The theory predicts that the "fittest" will produce the most offspring, and the definition of "fittest" is the one that produces the most offspring. Thus what the theory is saying is: "The one that produces the most offspring [fittest] will produce the most offspring." It is like asking someone, "Why does it rain," and the response being, "It rains because it rains." How this holds up as science is amazing!

Mathematical Challenges:

Mathematically, evolution via blind Natural Selection is an impossibility. For a worm to be formed from an amoeba, the alterations needed in its genetic code, would take 10 Trillion years to produce at the of 1 change per second (this is 500 times the age of the observable Universe). The number of alterations in genetic code needed for an ape to evolve into a man amount to 3×10^{520} changes. This is such a big impossibility that for example consider the volume of the entire Universe in terms of the diameter of ONE ELECTRON-one tiny electron much smaller than an atom is 10^{124} [Paul S Moorhead and Martin M Kaplan, *Mathematical challenges to the Neo-Darwinian interpretations of evolution*. Philadelphia, Wistar Institute Press].

> "The mathematician D.S Ulam argued that it was highly improbably that the eye could have evolved by the accumulation of small mutations because the number of mutations would have to be so large and the time available not nearly long enough for them to appear...a French Mathematician named Schutzenberger concluded that " there is a considerable gap in the neo-Darwinian theory of evolution, and we believe the gap to be of such nature that it cannot be bridged with the current conception of biology." (Johnson 1993:38-39)

The Finch's Beak:

A blind process like Natural Selection cannot explain directed adaptation as is revealed in nature. Direction by itself whether it be environmental or internal to the organism, implies the existence of a directing mind. Any automatic system, which alters itself based on any stimuli, or any stimuli that direct change in a specific direction, exists only if a "recognizer" previously recognized a need and apparatus to deal with it were provided, or that nature is the apparatus that directs in a specific way based on laws that imply intelligence. The ability to adapt and to encourage adaptation in a particular direction is ingrained in the species or the environment by an intelligence that pre-recognized that such conditions could be faced by that species, or according to a specific organizational plan provided for the species. It is anything but blind, the end results prove that.

Go around a garden in the spring and see all the flowers growing and occupying the same niche. Some of them would have four or five or six petals. How can you prove the advantages of having four instead of five petals and so on? Why do they all flourish if Natural Selection ensures the survival of the fittest?

On one of the Hawaiian Islands, there are 300 species of Drosphilia, compared with only a half a dozen species in the neighboring Island. What this suggests is not slow sluggish Natural Selection but an "abrupt" genetic change quite different to the accumulation of minute changes as proposed by Darwin and his modern disciple Dawkins.

Competition or Non-competition:

The picture in nature of competition that Darwin envisioned is faulty also. His example of competition was that of a wolf. The wolf he said, that ran faster would kill more effectively and get the meat as compared to other wolves. Coming from a naturalist this conclusion is completely dishonest. Wolves, it has been observed, hunt in packs and SHARE the meat. It is also a well-known fact to naturalists that competition in the natural world is rare and animals have mechanisms like specialization of diet and defining of territories to avoid competition. Examples exist of fishes of various different species, recorded and video taped, which feed on the same coral reef in close proximity to each other without any conflict whatsoever. P.P Grasse, the French biologist studied butterflies and found no competition among them.

Evolutionists suggest that "wings" got developed as an advantage. If flight was such an advantage why do we see penguins trying to give up that advantage and return to its ancestral marine life, from which they emerged according to evolutionary theory? Other valid questions that arise are: Who evolved from whom? In terms of color and art, the butterfly is much superior to the human. In terms of memory retention as a function of brain weight, the Dolphin exceeds all. The termite, smaller than an ant, in terms of warfare and the poison that it produces is much more effective than bigger so-called higher stage in evolution—animals. In terms of radar vision, the bat is unsurpassed.

"O humankind, an example is struck so pay attention to it: Those on whom you call besides God will never be able to create a fly even though they combine together for the purpose..... So weak are the seeker and the sought." Koran 22:73

Self-destruct?

It is a well-known fact that certain conifer plants produce chemical compounds that irresistibly attract coleoptera which then devour them. The production of these chemical compounds is therefore responsible for the death of this plant. This process has been going on for millions of years. Where has Natural Selection vanished in the case of this poor plant. There are species of the antelope whose hoofs contain glands which secrete a particular odor, which as the antelope runs is left on the ground and makes the attacking carnivore track it. Thus, here is another case of Natural Selection taking a vacation.

Catastrophe or Gradual Extinction?

Evolution by Natural Selection implies a gradual extinction. The fittest survive and the weak are gradually wiped out. As a result it predicts the multiplicity of fossils showing intermediaries between the various stages of evolution [the famous "missing links"]. Not only does the fossil record not show gradual evolution as envisioned by Darwin, it shows sudden *extinction* that is a problem from Darwinism.

> *"...There appear to have been a number of mass extinctions in the history of the earth, and debate still continues about what caused them. Two catastrophes in particular stand out: the Permian extinction of about 245 million years ago, which exterminated half the families of marine invertebrates and probably more than 90% of all species; and the famous "K-T" extinction at the end of the Cretaceous era, about 65 million ago, which exterminated the dinosaurs and a great deal else besides, including those ammonites whose disappearance*

Darwin conceded to have been wonderfully sudden." (Johnson 1993:57).
"If God wills He can destroy you and produce a new creation. That is not difficult for God (Koran)"

Homology as Proof of Macroevolution: Not!

Darwin concluded that since similarities exist in organisms belonging to different species regardless of their habits of life, therefore all species MUST have a common ancestor. Indeed, homology, as he defined it, was what he took most comfort in defending his theory.

What he might not have realized is that the above is "his" interpretation of homology and not a strong scientific conclusion. If I see the Mercedes insignia on all different models of Mercedes, would I conclude that they all have a common ancestor? No, I would conclude that they have the same manufacturer, who builds them according to a blue print and signs his or her name. Darwin's conclusion was at best subjective. I could say that the Creator has a pattern or method of creation, his signature that proves one as against many creators. Why would my conclusion be wrong?

Invoking homology is taking refuge in a philosophical argument. If Darwinism is to be seen as a science, it has to provide empirical evidence. Long before Darwin, taxonomists had recognized the idea of homology, their philosophical explanation was different but philosophically it was as sound as Darwin's explanation. We need empirical evidence to take a theory from the realm of philosophy to the level of science. Darwin acknowledged that empirical evidence was missing in the case of his theory but then when objections arose he resorted to rhetorical rebuttals, having nothing to do with empirical scientific evidence.

The homology that Darwin pointed out was based on the pentadectyl (5 fingers) pattern of the hind limb, showing similarities in the early embryo of the Kangaroo, who uses these for jumping, in the Koala who uses them for leaf eating and others. Darwin had no idea of genetics, advances in which were made much after his passing away. If it was shown that homologous genes specified homologous structures and if embryological research showed that homologous structures followed similar development patters then he might have had a case. However, it has been clearly shown today that homologous structures are inspired by non-homologous genetic systems. The origin of homologous structures is not homologous at all. In embryology, the difference between the division of egg to the blastula and the blastula itself is very different when compared between amphibian, reptile and mammal. Also the way in which the gastrula gets formed. If classification was done solely on embryology then these structures could never have been termed homologous since they are arrived at by different routes.

Consider another example from botany; Conifers and Angiosperms are considered as homologous but they differ markedly in the way the ovule and the endosperm forms. Darwin was completely wrong when he suggested in his definition of homology as, *"relationship between parts which result from their development from corresponding embryonic parts." (On The Origin of Species, page 492).*

De Beer, British embryologist and the Director of the British Natural History Museum, in his article, Homology the Unresolved Problem (1971:15) writes:

> *"Homologous structures need not be controlled by identical genes and homology of phenotype does not imply similarity of genotype."*

Almost every gene that has been studied in animals has been found to affect more than one organ system. A multiple effect known as Pleiotrophy. What really debunks Darwinism and his homology argument is that Pleiotrophic effects are invariably <u>species specific</u>. Also according to basic biochemical design no species can be thought of as being primitive and ancestral with respect to any other species. How biochemical systems evolved remains a mystery and a "area of silence" for Darwinians. There is almost complete silence in biochemical literature and journals discussing the evolutionary pathway leading to the development of biochemical systems (Behe 1996).

"Although it is true that vertebrates all pass through an embryonic stage at which they resemble each other, in fact they develop to this stage very differently. After a vertebrate egg is fertilized, it undergoes cell divisions and cell movements characteristic of its class: fishes follow one pattern, amphibians another one, birds yet another, and mammals still another. The differences cannot be explained as larval adaptations, since these early stages occur before the larvae form and thus are apparently not exposed to Natural Selection."
(Johnson 1993:73)

Darwin's subjective argument concerning homology (which he considered one of his strongest cases for evolution by Natural Selection) is further disproved by the existence of homologous phenotypes that can by no stretch of the imagination be attributed to a common ancestor via Natural Selection. Consider the forelimb, which in the early development is also based on the pentadectyl patter and cannot be distinguished from the hind limb. Yet it cannot be said that the hind limb evolved from the fore or vice versa. According to evolutionary theory, the forelimb arose from the pectoral fin of the fish and the hind from the pelvic fin, and also the final structure in adults of the fore and the hind are markedly different.

Evolutionists tend to judge overall similarity on terms of skeletal anatomy [especially when they suggest the evolution of the mammals from reptiles, Therapsida]. This however is faulty. There is, for example, an almost identical convergence between the marsupial and the placental dogs of Australia. They are incredibly similar in gross appearance and skeletal structure, teeth, skull etc. So similar in fact that only a skilled zoologist can distinguish between them. Yet in terms of their soft anatomy, there is an enormous difference between the two. Also consider the case of the whales, fish and ichthyosaurs, the similarity of forelimb of mole and the insect mole cricket, the design of the eye of the invertebrates and cephalopods and the cochlea in birds and mammals. However these small similarities do not imply any close biological relationship at all!

There is not one iota of evidence to suggest that one species of hominid evolved into another via Natural Selection. The existence (of some hominid species) has been determined, one species disappears and the other SUCCEEDS it. There is however no scientific evidence to defend the theory that man [Homo Sapiens] are descended from great apes, via blind Natural Selection.

> "If (God) wills, He destroys you and in your place appoints whom He wills as <u>successors</u> just as He brought you forth from the descendants of other peoples." Koran 6:133
>
> "Indeed, We created them and strengthened them. And when We willed, We replaced them completely by people of the same kind." Koran 76:28

The waves of hominids appear as <u>successors</u> one of the other. They represent stages [or phases] in succession each one showing a progression in intelligence and psychical powers—an increasingly sophisticated organization of the brain.

> "And He [God] created you in stages [or phases]." Koran 71:14

Neo-Darwinians claim that birds evolved from reptiles. However the facts point out that whenever we have ever uncovered the first representatives of a group for example the bird, the fossil records show a construction that is highly specialized and completely characteristic of the whole group. The fact is that every single flying bird from the Archaeopteryx on has possessed highly developed aerofoil (flight wings) containing fully developed flight feathers. It shows that the one who designed these has a full awareness of the laws of aerodynamics. Blind, Natural Selection based on survival of the fittest could never achieve this. The sudden origin of the angiosperm for example and the first animals in Cambrian rocks has baffled biologists.

So big is the gap between species, that not only is there no empirical evidence linking the species but also transitional hypothetical intermediary groups cannot even be constructed by Neo-Darwinians. Considering these facts it is a surprise that the scientific community even listens to them.

Darwinists say that the purpose of evolution is to attain survival adaptation. Adaptation, without any intelligence involved, based on random chance does not make any sense at all. The concept of what is "functional" has to be defined [using intelligence] and then strides towards reaching that goal made. Without putting "intelligence" in the picture, this journey to perfect adaptation makes no sense at all.

As an example, take the claim that birds evolved from reptiles and the reptile scale led to the development of the highly specialized wing of the bird. Some Darwinians suggest that the wing developed out of an intermediary structure of "gliding" device. They do not realize however that according to their theory a need must be met for "further" improvement by Natural Selection to ensure survival. If it was a gliding device, then to be a good gliding device it had to have as a principle air trapping by making the surface area big. Any fraying of the reptile scales in a move towards wings would make them pervious to the air and much less useful as gliding devices. Being aware of this problem some Darwinians have suggested that the wing developed out of insect eating reptiles having a need to "net" the insects with their scales, which led to the formation of wings. Any net however has to be pervious to air for it to be useful. Any wings pervious to air would be useless for flight. You cannot have it both ways.

Evolutionists pointed to organs, which they termed as useless in the human body as evidence of remains from a lower evolutionary form. However those same organs that they pointed to as being useless [thymus, pineal gland, tonsils, the appendix] have all been shown to be very useful in the human body according to modern research, playing a big role even in the human body's fight against cancer.

Darwin Falsified:

On Page 182 of *On the Origin of Species,* Darwin writes:
> "If it could be demonstrated that any complex organ existed which could not possibly have been formed by numerous successive slight modifications, MY THEORY WOULD ABSOLUTELY BREAK DOWN."

Consider a modern day disciple of Darwin, Dawkins, on page 91 of his book, *"The Blind Watchmaker,"* writes,
> "I do not believe that such a case (of a complex organ that cannot be produced by slight modification) will ever be found. If it is... *I shall cease to believe in Darwinism.*"

Now consider these examples among the numerous that exist:

The flight feather of the Bird:

> "Have you not seen the Birds that are subjected (to God's command) in the air of the sky? Surely in this are signs for a people who confirm." (Koran 16:79)

Each wing of every species of bird consists of a central shaft carrying a series of barbs, which are positioned at right angles to the shaft to form a vane. The wing is designed by someone who is well aware of the laws of aerodynamics and the problems that might arise during flight. One of the problems of all aerofoils is turbulence, which reduces lift and causes stalling. Turbulence is cut down by providing slots in the aerofoil to let through part of the air stream and smooth the flow. Aero-engineers use this same principle in designing airplanes. Surprisingly enough, the wings of the birds have this already built in. Consider the flight of the hummingbird to appreciate how complex the properties of the feathered aerofoil really is.

Just how the scales of reptiles led to the development via blind Natural Selection, to such a complex structure, as the wing remains an enigma to biologists. No one has come close even to describing the stages (intermediary) and what functionality they would serve and how they would arise. We are thus at an absence of even a theoretic basis for such a 'fantastic' idea.

Bird Respiration:

Not only is the wing that is unique and uniform throughout all species of birds, they have another unique feature and that is their respiratory system. In all vertebrates (those having backbones), air is drawn into the lungs via branching tubes which end in air sacs. Therefore air flows in and out through the same passage. In birds however, the flow of air is unidirectional. The bronchi break down into para-bronchi, which permeate the whole lung and reconnect again to form a complete circulatory system.

How such a system could have evolved via Natural Selection is simply impossible. The slightest alteration in functioning of respiration leads to immediate death. The system appears uniform in all birds in a fully functional form. We have yet to see any Darwinian set up a theory even of how this modification took place from the reptile. In the absence of even a theory on how it happened and absolutely no empirical evidence, we are justified to state that Darwin and Dawkins have been falsified.

The Bones:

Consider the construction of bones. Without them many terrestrial creatures couldn't support themselves against the drag of gravity. Their construction shows a unique design of spaces left for blood vessels and bone making cells. The major bones contain a cavity lined with a sheath, which generates blood cells. Without newer cells being made all the time we would die, as human blood cells have a life of only 120 days. The joints are another wonder with a lubricant, the synovial fluid. Nothing as complex as this structure can arise due to accumulation of chance mutations. It would require a burst of DIRECTED mutations, all integrated to a single end. Natural Selection cannot explain this or any other similar complex structure.

Immune and Blood Clotting Systems:

The immune and blood clotting mechanisms in organisms whereby foreign intruders are detected and the organism is saved from bleeding to death respectively, can truly be defined as "Irreducibly complex" systems. Just like a mouse trap will not work if any one of its parts is missing or is improperly placed, the system of chain reactions in blood clotting for example wont work if any part of the mechanism is crude.

Blood clotting works by turning on and off of proteins at precisely the correct spot at the correct time. If anything goes wrong in the process if the proteins are crudely made or improper inhibitors present, the organism would either bleed to death or his whole blood would clot and kill him or the clot would form at the wrong spot and block circulation and cause heart failure. How such a system could have arisen out of blind Natural Selection remains an enigma to this date to biochemists.

> *"By irreducibly complex I mean a single system composed of several well-matched, integrating parts that contribute to the basic function, wherein the removal of any one of the parts causes the system to effectively cease functioning." (Behe 1996:39)*

Transcription System:

The protein manufacturing system of all cells requires the integrated activity of nearly 100 different proteins, all carrying out different but specific steps in the assembly of a new protein molecule. If only a small proportion of these were "crudely made" as evolutionists would suggests in the earlier stages of the cell, it is practically impossible for any protein to ever be manufactured let alone with a specific configuration of molecules capable of performing specific functions.

The translation system in a cell is completely dependent on accurately made proteins and an imperfect protein synthetic system is hard even to theorize. It would sound like an unintelligent and absurd hypothesis to a geneticist. Just how efficient enzymes could have been manufactured before an efficient translation system (as evolutionists claim) remains an enigma to them to this day and sounds like gibberish to the objective geneticist.

The bigger problem, even bigger than the one above is that the protein synthetic system cannot work in isolation but only in conjunction with other complex subsystems of the cell. Thus the origin of the replication mechanism cannot be envisioned via Natural Selection.

Concludes Behe (1996):

> "Molecular evolution is not based on scientific authority. There is no publication in the scientific literature—in prestigious journals, specialty journals, or books—that describes how molecular evolution of any real, complex, biochemical system either did occur or even might have occurred...absolutely NONE are supported by pertinent experiments or calculations..." (Behe 1996:185)

The Originator of the Genetic Code Makes the Change:

> "...There's no changing what Allah [God] creates. That is the established standard system/order, but most among humankind know not." (Koran 30:30)

Nilson Heribert of the University of Lund, Sweden states:

> "Species are types that do not change and cannot change."

Genetic engineering distorts or repairs what has been distorted of a given system. It cannot change species on a grand scale. It operates within the boundaries contained in the system. The above verse of the Koran and the quote by Nilson Heribert state the same thing. There is "intelligence" involved and not blind Natural Selection alone.

> "The results of these cumulative efforts [to uncover the complexity of the cell] at the molecular level—is a loud, clear, piercing cry of "design?" The result is so unambiguous and so significant that it must be ranked as one of the greatest achievements in the history of science." (Behe 1996:232-233)

Directed Evolution and not Natural Selection:

> "He is Allah (God), the Creator, the <u>Evolver</u> (Koran)."
>
> "The fact that all living organism are now known to be specified in the linear DNA sequence…has presented science with a new and utterly different representation of the organic world. These discoveries imply that not only is DNA remarkably fit for its hereditary role, it is also remarkably fit in a number of different ways for directed evolution." (Denton 1998:275)

Behe states about empirical evidence:

> "Modern biochemistry routinely designs biochemical systems, which are now known to be the basis of life. Therefore we do have experience in observing the INTELLIGENT DESIGN of the components of life." (Behe 1996: 219)

Nature's Destiny:

> "…The conclusion to design is not based on evidence that the laws of nature are adapted to some degree for life (to emerge) but rather on the far stronger case that the cosmos is optimally adapted for life so that <u>EVERY</u> constituent of the cell and <u>EVERY</u> law of nature is uniquely and ideally fashioned to that end." (Denton 1998:385)

One statement captures it all, centuries earlier:

> Do they [the disbelievers] not see that God has subjected for them <u>WHATSOEVER</u> is in the heavens and the earth…? (KORAN 31:20)

There are many modern-day biologists who do not accept Evolution by Natural Selection as a fact because they recognize that empirical evidence is missing and that there are too many flaws and "missing links," and bad reasoning. Frustrated by the evidence, Francis Crick, the co-discoverer of DNA envisioned life arriving on earth from a different planet [as the origin of life on earth cannot be explained by leaving God out of the picture]. His theory is called "directed panspermia." This general idea seems to be based on the comic character Superman. An advanced civilization, facing extinction sent primitive life forms to earth in a spaceship. The primitive forms appear "suddenly" on earth.

Whereas, we can construct a theory to "fit" some of the facts, this theory [about spacemen] cannot be tested just like Natural Selection. The "home planet" is extinct according to the theory and the "spacemen" are just as invisible as the "missing links" in the evolutionary chain of Darwin (Johnson 1993:110).

It is unfortunate that based on blind materialism we base our entire knowledge of the origin of species, biology and medicine on the "fairy tale", termed Evolution by Natural Selection. I end with what Johnson writes:

> "When a scientist of Crick's caliber [the co-discoverer of the structure of DNA] feels he has to invoke invisible spacemen, it is time to consider whether the field of pre-biological evolution has come to a dead end..." (Johnson 1993:111)
>
> "The most of them follow nothing but conjecture. And surely, conjecture can never take the place of truth. Indeed, Allah [God] is aware of what they do." Koran 10:36
>
> "O Humankind what has deceived you concerning your Cherisher (God), Most Bountiful, Who created you, then fashioned, then proportioned you. Into whatever form He wills He makes you.." Koran 82:6-8

God, the Genetic Code and the Koran:

> *"By the Glorious Koran! Nay, but they are amazed that a Warner of their own has come unto them. And the rejecters say: ` This is a strange thing: when we are dead and have become dust (shall we be made alive again)? That would be a return most distant.' We know that which the earth takes of them, and with Us is a protected transcription [or writing—Kitaab]. Nay, but they have denied the truth when it came to them, therefore now, they are in a troubled case..." Koran 50:2-5*

What is this protected transcription?

The protected transcription from which the human being can again be recreated [the context of the verse] after his/her death is the genetic code. Russian scientists recently discussed reproducing an extinct species of elephant by the use of a microscopic unit of a long dead gene material. No one said that such an attempt was unreasonable. It is perfectly logical, yet they have not been able to do it.

However, when it comes to the Koran, and when the same terminology is used, centuries ago, the rejecters say it's unreasonable! It may be unusual but it certainly is not unreasonable. Indeed, such evidence in the Koran, considering the time of its revelation proves it, in accordance with its claims, of originating with the one who has knowledge of creation.

> *Clone: a group of genetically identical cells or whole organisms derived from a single cell or organism. Clones arise naturally in a number of ways. The body of an adult animal or plant is typically a clone of cells having arisen by mitosis from a single cell, the fertilized egg.... The cloning of mammals, including man is theoretically possible, but it is more difficult to achieve because of the smaller size of mammalian egg and the more complex conditions required for normal embryonic development. [From Encyclopedia Americana, volume 7, 1993]*

The Koran, over 1400 years before the above article was written compared the stages of human embryology [before the discovery of the microscope] to the resurrection of the long dead on the last day for judgment [a concept involving cloning]:

> "What, does humankind think that they will be left aimless? Was he [she] not a drop ejaculated? Then he was a leech like structure. And He [God] created and formed. And made of him a pair, the male and the female. What, is He not then able to quicken the dead?" Koran 75:36-40

The above verse questions those who reject the notion of the resurrection of the dead. Which is the more difficult task: That you were created from an insignificant drop, which was so small that it couldn't be seen without a microscope, or that some day you will be formed again from your remnants?

> "Your creation and your resurrection [on the last day] is as a single unit [nafs—one substance or essence]." Koran 31:28

Cloning involves the derivation of a group of genetically identical cells or whole organism from a single [Waahid—in the verse above] original cell or organism.

> "Say: If the sea were to become ink for the words of my Cherisher (God), indeed the sea would be used up before the words of my Cherisher (God) were exhausted, even though we brought the like of it [i.e. another sea] to its aid." Koran 18:109

Literally:

> "At the moment of conception, when a sperm and ovum (egg) unite, an incredible number of personal features and growth patterns are determined. It is estimated that the genetic information carried in each human cell would fill thousands of 1000—page books—and that's in fine print." (Coon :366).

"A recent editorial in the "Science" journal, titled, "Hints of a language in junk DNA (Nov 25, 1994), describing the work of Eugene Stanley of Boston University, who used statistical techniques borrowed from linguists and found evidence that much of the non protein coating DNA has informational characteristics resembling those of human language." (Denton 1998:290)

The above Koranic verse is proven true literally if we consider all the cells making up creation. If all the information contained in all the cells were to be written down, surely: *"…the sea would be exhausted before the words of the Cherisher (God) are exhausted."* Consider this: one cell can fill up thousands of 1000—page books and that is in fine print!

Note:

This paper <u>DOES NOT</u> present in any way the Christian Creationists position on humankind's origin. The Koran does not set a time of 6000 years for the creation of the world neither does it support the unscientific ideas in the Bible. The Koran does not validate the Bible nor the scientific errors contained in the Bible

Bibliography:

Asadi, Muhammed A. Koran: A Scientific Analysis. Lahore, Pakistan 1992
Behe, Michael. Darwin's Black Box. 1996. The Free Press.
Bucaille, Maurice. What is the Origin of Man. Seghers. Paris 1987.
Coon, Dennis. Introduction to Psychology. 5th Ed, West Publishing Co. 1989.
Denton, Michael. Evolution: A Theory in Crisis. 1984: The Free Press
Denton, Michael J. Nature's Destiny. 1998. New York: The Free Press.
Darwin: The Origin of Species.
Dawkins, Richard. The Blind Watchmaker. W.W Norton & Co. 1996.

Johnson. Phillip. Darwin on Trial. 2nd ed.1993. Inter-varsity Press: Illinois.

Koran—Translation from the original Arabic.

Encyclopedia Americana, vol. 7, 1993.

Guyton, Arthur C. Physiology of the Human Body. 6th edition. Holt Saunders International Editions.

Moore, Keith L. Before we are born: Basic Embryology & Birth Defects. 2nd edition.

W. B. Saunders Co, Philadelphia 1983.

Moore, K. L. A Scientists Interpretation of references to Embryology in Al—Qur'an. 1986.

Nurbaki, Haluk Dr. Verses from the Koran & Facts of Science. Ankara, Turkey 1989

Taylor, Gordon Rattray. The Great Evolutionary Mystery. Harper & Row, NY 1983

KORAN & THE BIOMEDICAL SCIENCES

"And He is aware of every creation."
(Koran 36:79)

Enumerated Exact Quotations and Documented Scientific Findings:

1). *"He [i.e. God] created you in the wombs of your mothers in three fold darkness"* (Koran 39:6).
The three fold darkness may refer to: i) Anterior abdominal wall; ii) The uterine wall & iii) Amnio Chronic membrane [Dr. Keith L. Moore—University of Toronto].

2). *"Then We [plural of majesty for God] placed him [i.e. man/woman] as a drop [Nutfa in Arabic] in a safe lodging. Then We made the drop [Nutfa] into a leech like structure [Alaca in Arabic]. Then out of the leech like structure, a chewed lump [Mudghah in Arabic]. Then out of the chewed lump bones, and We clothed the bones in flesh. Then we developed out of it another creature. Therefore, blessed be Allah [God], the best of those that create"* (Koran 23: 13-14)

ANALYSIS OF KORAN 23:14

i) *"We placed him as a drop in a safe lodging".*
The drop [Zygote] divides to form a blastocyst which is implanted in a safe lodging [Uterus].

ii) *"Then We made the drop into a leech like structure (Alaca)".*
The human embryo [days 7-24] looks and behaves like a leech. Just as a leech derives blood from the host, the embryo derives blood from the

pregnant endometrium [or decidua]. The embryo of 23-24 days, in its appearance remarkably resembles a leech. As there were no microscopes available 1400 years back such a statement in the Koran is rather fascinating indeed. [Adapted from Keith L. Moore]

iii) *"Then out of the leech like structure, we made a chewed lump [Mudghah in Arabic]"*

In Arabic *Mudghah* signifies chewed lump or chewed flesh. This is stated in contrast to intact flesh, which is signified by the word *Laham* [in Arabic].

Towards the end of the 4th week, the human embryo looks like a chewed lump of flesh. The chewed appearance results from somites, which resemble teeth marks. [Keith L. Moore]

iv) *"Then out of the chewed lump, bones, and then We clothed the bones in flesh"*

This is in accord with embryological development. First bones form as cartilage models and then muscles [flesh] develop around them from the somatic mesoderm. [Keith L. Moore]

v) *"Then We develop out of it another creature"*

After the formation of bones and muscles, by the end of the 8th week, the embryo has distinctive human characteristics and is called a fetus [refers to "another creature"].

3) *"O mankind! if you are in doubt concerning the resurrection then Indeed, We have created you from dust, then from a drop [Nutfa], then from a leech like structure [Alaca], then from a chewed lump of flesh [Mudghah], partly formed and partly unformed..."*(Koran 22:5)

The statement "partly formed and partly unformed" may indicate that the embryo is composed of both differentiated and undifferentiated tissue. [Keith L. Moore]

When cartilage bones are differentiated, the embryonic connective tissue [mesenchyme] around them is undifferentiated.

4) *"And He [Allah or God] it is who created Mankind of water"* (Koran 25:54).

The Ovum cell from which the human being is created has as its main functioning portion the cytoplasm, which is between 70% to 85% water.

5) *"And He [Allah or God] created the two pairs male and female from an ejaculated drop"* (Koran 53:45,46)

The male sperm is the "ejaculated drop". Females do not possess ejaculated semen. The male sperm carrying the Y—chromosome determines sex. Therefore, the ejaculated drop determines sex. There were no microscopes to have knowledge of this 1400 years back, the time of the Koranic revelation.

6) *"Surely, We created man from a mixed (Amshaj in Arabic) drop.."* (Koran 76:2)

The Zygote (drop) forms by the union of mixtures of the sperm and the ovum.

7) *"…And He (God) gave you hearing and sight and feeling and understanding.."* (Koran 32:9).

The above verse has as its context the creation of mankind. The special senses of hearing, seeing and feeling develop in the exact same order as mentioned in the above verse. The primordia of the internal ears appear before the beginning of the eyes, and the brain [the site of feeling and understanding] differentiates last.

> *"The Koran describes not only the development of external form but emphasizes also the internal stages—the stages inside the embryo of its creation and development, emphasizing major events recognized by contemporary science…If I was to transpose myself into that era, knowing what I do today and describing things, I could not describe the things that were described…I see no evidence to refute the concept that this individual Muhammed had to be developing this information from some place…so I see nothing in conflict with the concept that divine intervention was involved…"*

(E. Marshall Johnson, Professor and Chair, Department of Anatomy, Daniel Bough Institute, Thomas Jefferson University, Philadelphia, Pennsylvania.)

II) Other data:

8) *"Surely those who disbelieve our signs, We shall burn them at a fire. As often as their skins are wholly burned, we shall give them in exchange other skins so that they may keep tasting the punishment [i.e. keep feeling the pain of burning]." (Koran 4:56)*

Full thickness burns destroy nerve endings so that further burning does not cause pain. The pin prick test is used to verify full thickness loss. The Koran informed us about this over 1400 years back when people knew nothing about full thickness and partial thickness burns and their anaesthetic effect.

9) *"...And you will see mankind on that day [i.e. the day of judgement] as drunken [intoxicated], yet they will not be drunken [intoxicated].." (Koran 22:2)*

Effects similar to intoxication can be produced in our bodies even though no intoxicant has been consumed [just as indicated by the above verse of the Koran]. Modern physiology has found this in the case of at least one pathological state, Mania [which involves feelings of intense euphoria and frenzied behavior].

10) *"We have charged the human that he/she be kind to his/her parents...his bearing and his weaning are thirty months. Then when he is fully developed and reaches FORTY YEARS.." (Koran 46:15)*

Psychological tests show that the overall quantity of stored knowledge in a person's mind increases during the first 39 years of his life, reaching a peak at this time (Guyton, page 207). The Koran said 40 years much before such psychological tests were conducted.

While commenting on the above verses of the Koran, please consider the fact that the Koran was revealed at a time period and place where

people had little, if any scientific knowledge and lacked the equipment to provide such accurate descriptions contained in the above verses.
References to the Koran e.g. 22:5 refer to Koran chapter (sura) 22, verse or sentence 5.

Bibliography:

1. Asadi, Muhammed A. Koran: A Scientific Analysis. Self published. Lahore 1992.
2. Guyton, Arthur C. Physiology of the Human Body. 6th edition. Holt Saunders International Editions.
3. Moore, Keith L. Before we are born: Basic Embryology & Birth Defects. 2nd edition.
W. B. Saunders Co, Philadelphia 1983.
4. Moore, K. L. A Scientists Interpretation of references to Embryology in Al—Qur'an. 1986.

KORAN & SCIENTIFIC SOCIOLOGY

"Look at the indicators of God's mercy [in the natural world], how He gives life to the earth after its death, most surely He will raise the dead to life again; and He has power over all things." (Koran 30:50)

The inspiration provided for social research in the Koran is the book's emphasis on a critical analysis of ideas and ideology. Ideas and ideology bred in ignorance lead, according to the Koran, to a social order that is contrary to the natural social order determined by the creator. A critical analysis is encouraged by the oft-repeated idea in the Koran that reason, rationality and empirical evidence (Koran 3:190-191), in short the method of science, is supreme in determining the truth, given how the human mind is designed to operate.

The Koran presents itself as a *"guide with evidence and a criterion"* (Koran 2:185) from the maker of all things to humankind, the bearer of God's trust on earth and maintainers of the "balance" (Koran 55:7-9) that God created. However, in "turning away" from that trust and "falling short" of the balance and "wasting by excess", humanity has created a multitude of social problems, problems that harm society in general and not only those who are directly responsible for them (Koran 8:25). It is not mystical determinism but "social" determinism that the Koran talks about (Koran 30:41). Consistent with this view, the Koran frequently mentions a "path" [*Sabeel* in Arabic] of various social actions leading to ends that are harmful or beneficial. This is somewhat similar to "Path Analysis" used by modern sociologists.

> "Behold! In the creation of the heavens and the earth; in the alternation of the night and day; in the sailing of the ships through the ocean for the benefit of mankind; in the rain which God sends down from the skies; and the life which He gives therewith to an earth that is dead; in the animals of all kinds that he scatters through the earth; in the change of winds and the clouds enslaved between the sky and the earth;—(here) indeed are signs for a discerning people." (Koran 2:164)

I realized during my research, in a manner similar to the evolution of the social sciences from the natural sciences, that if the method of science could be used to scrutinize and analyze the Koran in issues involving processes of nature and the natural world, the same could be applied regarding society. Debate about various social issues is common in the media today and more often than not, "religious" ideas regarding them are scoffed at as being unscientific and primitive. Contrary to this popular view, very early on in my readings of the Koran, I discovered an amazing congruence between modern scientific criteria and the Koran. For example, innovative medical drugs whose "benefits are less than their harmful side effects" are banned from marketing by the *Food and Drug Administration* in the United States. The Koran stated similar criteria as justification for prohibiting alcohol and other intoxicating drugs, centuries earlier:

> "They ask you concerning intoxicants and gambling. Say to them, in them are great harms and only some benefits for humankind; But the harm of them is much greater than their usefulness." (Koran 2:219)

My scientific analysis of the Koran continued while attending Southwest Missouri State University, in Springfield, Missouri. I made sure that every scientific paper I wrote incorporated in it ideas from the

Koran related to the topic of research. A few of my professors, who were patient and open-minded regarding my work, realized that agreed upon criteria, i.e. objective standards could be used to debate culture and values, scientifically. Sociologists nowadays almost all recognize this (Babbie 1992) though some "dogmatically" charge their science and in the process lose the essence of the scientific method itself. Thus, their use of the label "science" while abandoning the principles of science can be termed a "religion". Using Weber's terminology, turned on its head, it's like being enchanted by the "disenchantment" of the world. In my studies, I try to take the Koran, and the ideas contained within it, as a system (<u>deen</u> in Arabic) and base its examination on the principles of science.

The social "case" of the Koran has been closed prematurely. My web articles and books, aim reopen that "case" and to reexamine the charges that have been leveled against it for centuries.

Consider this small chapter (*Sura*) in the Koran:

"Have you seen the one who consciously denies the system [of the Koran]?
It is he who will repel the orphans and will urge not the feeding of the needy.
Woe unto those who worship, yet are heedless of the purpose of it;
Who would be seen at worship but refuse even <u>small necessities</u> to the needy?"
(Koran 107:1-7)

"Have you seen," implies an *empirical* verification of, as the sentence continues, the behavior of those who deny the system of the Koran, and those who do not deny it in public but in essence. As empirical evidence of this statement, consider the fact that over 30,000 children die every day on earth by causes that are preventable (UN Human Development Report 2000). In most instances these casualties result because of non-availability of "basic necessities" because of distribution mismatch, perpetuated by capitalism. Now consider the elite who controls these resources and their "conscious rejection" of the Koranic system of equitable distribution of wealth, based upon *Zakah*. *Zakah* implies a redistribution of 50% of the surplus of every Muslim that is beyond legitimate need, in the form of a social fund that removes iniquities in wealth distribution in society (Koran 59:7). This percentage is much greater than the 20/20 that the United Nations envisions.

As empirical evidence of the second part consider those that are labeled "Muslims", those who are often "seen" at worship five times a day, but remain ignorant of the social consciousness that prayer is supposed to inculcate in a believer. In many "Muslim" lands people starve or die of preventable causes because "small necessities" aren't available, yet the "Muslim" elites in these countries support a life style more conspicuous than those in most rich industrialized nations.

This was a small example of how the Koran approaches the study of individual and group behavior. Social research through operationalization of concepts, on a local or a global scale can provide for empirical testing of the Koran's statements. By making empirical observation the heart of its conclusions, the Koran encourages value-free positive sociology and acceptance that is based on confirmation (*sadq* in Arabic) and not on unreasoned faith at all. The concept of dogmatic "religion" and "blind faith", as understood by Western, English-speaking people, is completely alien to the Koran.

Following the example of the Koran, Ibn Khaldun (732-808) recognized as the founder of Sociology,

> *"Emphasized the necessity of subjecting both social and historical phenomena to scientific and objective analysis. He noted that those phenomena were not the outcome of chance, but were controlled by laws of their own, laws that had to be discovered and applied in the study of society, civilization and history. He remarked that historians have committed errors in their study of historical events, due to three major factors: (1) Their ignorance of the natures of civilization and*

people, (2) their bias and prejudice, and (3) their blind acceptance of reports given by others."(Zahoor 1996)

Thirteen centuries before Karl Marx (1818-1887) made a broad statement about religion as the *"opium of the masses"*; the Koran came to an empirical conclusion regarding the "use" of religion by the elite. In the following statement of the Koran, it is clearly stated that some groups, to further their economic causes, use religion:

"Woe to those who write the book with their own hands and then say, "This is from God," that they may exchange it for some miserable economic gain. Woe to them for what their hands do write and woe to them for what they earn therewith." (Koran 2:79)

It is not only the interpretation of religion but also the interpretation of science as well, what we call pseudo-science, which can become the "opium of the masses"

Fourteen centuries before Edward O. Wilson (1929-), working as a Naturalist particularly with ants, arrived at his version of Sociobiology, the Koran contained this statement:

"There is not an animal on earth nor the birds that fly with their wings, but are <u>communities</u> like unto you. We have neglected nothing in the book..." (Koran 6:38)

All through the Koran is recognition of sociological factors that keep people away from God and His message. Factors like group-solidarity, tradition, the pride in social position, social stratification etc. Mentioned together with these is the social psychology of those who refuse God and the cultural reasons on why they refuse, as are economic considerations and their effects on behavior and society. Things like, "being seduced by the life of the world," "not looking beyond their material existence," "being overly engrossed in their competition for the material goods of this life," "staying away from spending because of an unreasonable fear of poverty" and "circuits of income." Competition, mutual rivalry and pride in possessions are described as motivators for individuals leading to a certain type of social behavior and a society that is contrary to the "ideal-type" desired by the Koran.

Consider this conclusion in the Koran, centuries before Vilfredo Pareto (1848-1923) outlined "elite theory":

"Thus are appointed in every city elite ones (Akabir in Arabic) of its malicious folk and they plot therein." (Koran 6:123)

C. Wright Mills (1916-1962), in his pioneering work, *The Power Elite* (1956), reached a similar conclusion as the Koran that has become the basis of countless sociological studies all across the field, including Urban Sociology. Note that the Koran mentions "every city" and not just one city and that it mentions decisions being made (plotting) by the elite that can have major consequences (see Koran 14:46). Compare what the Koran says to what C. Wright Mills wrote in 1956:

"The power elite is composed of men whose positions enable them to transcend the ordinary environment of ordinary men and women: they are in a position to make major decisions having major consequences." (Mills 1956:3-4)

Thirteen centuries before Emile Durkheim (1858-1917) used the term *Social Fact* to describe the objective realities of society that are external to the individuals, yet directs their behavior, and developed the concept of the *collective conscience*, the Koran concluded:

"Thus unto <u>every nation</u> have We made their doings seem fair. Then unto their Lord is their return, and He will tell them what they used to do. " (Koran 6:108).

The Koran mentions an accurate description of life, the life-world (<u>hayat ud dunya</u> in Arabic) being similar to a play or a game (<u>Llaib</u> in Arabic), in which the actors are busy with "passions, pageantry, mutual rivalry and boasting among themselves in terms of possessions and progeny" (Koran 57:20). The Koran conceptualized this, at least fourteen centuries before sociologist *Erving Goffman* (1922-1982) popularized a particular type of *interactionist* model, the *dramaturgical approach* that takes a similar view of life (Schaefer & Lamm 1998:24).

The Koran mentions the *world's life* and its created culture as an "illusion" (Koran 57:20). An illusion that projects an image of permanence yet is transitory, and an illusion that directs people to accept something as real, which in reality is engineered, and unreal. This is similar to *'life-world'* and its colonization, discussed by Jurgen Habermas (1929-), yet it predates his work by fourteen centuries. The elite and a state controlled by them thus emerges as a creator of culture(s) by shaping the 'life-world' of individuals, projected in the form of a society that best serves their interests.

> *"Illusion is an important device in the arsenal of the masters of capitalism. Their futures are built almost entirely on illusion: the illusion of white supremacy, the illusion of democracy, the illusion of fair and free elections, the illusion of free speech, a free press, and the illusion of a sound economy." (Chinyelu 1999:62)*

The elite [*akabir* in Arabic] not only creates culture by their control of the diffusion of ideas in society, by their monopoly over "persuasion resources", they directly create culture by their design and use of space. Space, how your cities, your neighborhoods, your organizations are constructed, designed and run all have a close connection to culture(s). City building needs resources and the elite controls these resources.

> *"In the history of the world, there has never been a propaganda effort to match that of advertising in the twentieth century. More thought, more effort, more money goes into advertising than has ever gone into any other campaign to change social consciousness." (Kilbourne 1999:75)*

By strategically displacing jobs and people and concentrating poverty in the inner cities, the elite, artificially install and nourish a "street code": A code that forces people, on a social level to adopt it as the only reality, if they are to survive. Sociologist Elijah Anderson in his book, *Code of the Street* (1999), states

> "It is nothing less than the cultural manifestation of persistent urban poverty. It is a mean adaptation to blocked opportunities and profound lack, a grotesque form of coping by young people constantly undermined by a social system that historically has limited their social options and until recently rejected their claims to full citizenship." (Anderson 1999:146-147)

Those who refuse to be "blinded" by such structural alienation are trapped by "chemical—alienation" through alcohol and drugs that directly produce an illusion of reality. As a result of all this artificially engineered culture, a "real world" much removed from the actual real world is projected. A world that traps people in a cycle from which escape becomes almost impossible. Alienation and anomie are closely linked. In this instant society, we have an *instant* anomie-producing instrument, alcohol.

> "Their example is as a mirage in a desert. The thirsty one supposes it to be water till he comes unto it and finds nothing...or as shadows upon a sea obscure: there covers them a wave, above which is a wave, above which are clouds; layer upon layer of darkness. When they hold out their hands, they almost cannot see them." (Koran 24:39-40)

Similar to the "initial conditions" studied by physicists, which led to the evolution of a particular type of Universe and the eventual emergence of life, without which the Universe would not have resembled what we see today and we wouldn't have been here to see it, the "initial conditions" in society that determine its structure are crucial to understanding the nature of interaction. This is in the tradition of Auguste Comte (1798-1857), the person who coined the term sociology and sought to model the discipline after the physical sciences, particularly physics (social physics).

The "initial conditions" in the physical sciences are mysterious and cannot be explained without reference to a designer, the odds of them occurring by chance equal zero by all real measures. Contrary to this, the intelligently set "initial conditions" that determines the economy and the relationships of production have human social origins and can be studied by historical and comparative analysis.

The scientific system demands replication, verification and falsification, hence empirical analysis should become an important part of any theoretical system. It is through empirical verification that workable theories can be extracted from ones that have at best metaphysical and rhetorical value.

In the past 20 to 30 years as progress has been made in the physical sciences, a hidden order has been revealed in nature. Physicists call this the *Cosmic Code*. It is an intelligently designed, normative order (the values of which can be derived by analogy) written in a language that humanity can understand, the language of mathematics. In attempting to understand this message, of which only a small part has been decoded yet, scientists aim to uncover a grand unifying theory of everything. Newtonian "positive" physics is just a small part of this normative (value) order called the *Theory of Everything*. Once this *Cosmic Code* is decoded, scientists envision linking all human knowledge together based on it. We will then be able to deduce from it the natural social order and understand the values based upon which "ideal" human societies can be created in reality, rather than the subjective abstractions that embody Max Weber's (1864-1920)"ideal types".

Contrary to the "natural order" conjectured by Herbert Spencer (1820-1903) in his Social Darwinism, which was natural only to the extent of a reproduction of a "social construction" of a particular type of status quo, the *Theory of Everything* will present objective reality of a normative and positive nature based on the larger scale governance of the Universe. It will transcend all societies.

Once this theory is understood, it can be speculated that all other systems of social organization based on inadequate and incomplete knowledge like Capitalism, Socialism, Communism, Anarchism and the other "isms" will become obsolete and outdated.

> *"Therefore, set your face to the system of Islam. The nature of God based upon which he has natured humankind. There is no altering what God creates. That is the established standard order. However most among humankind understand not (Koran 30:30)."*

The Koran is not about "self-righteousness," as writings on what is popularly termed as a "religious" source are often accused of being. Theory and action need to be separated for the purpose of pure research. Thus we need to test the Koran by its claims and not by the actions of those who claim to believe in it or follow it.

Not only is the Koran written in the most mathematical/logical of all human languages—Arabic, it is unique in history in that it led to the development of the rules of that language itself. While Bertrand Russell envisioned creating a logical/mathematical language, the Koran did that factually fourteen centuries back. No other book in the history of the world has "invented" the rules of a language, so to speak, as the Koran did when it gave birth to the rules governing written Arabic. Thus Arabic may be described as the ideal "human" language (based upon Russell's criteria) that comes closest to emulating the mathematical language of the Universe, in an objective fashion based on its logical foundations, which even the lay person can understand. We need to ask here, could a man who had no formal schooling, *Muhmmed ibn Abdullah*, and lived fourteen centuries back, have done this?

> *"Arabic most precise and primitive of the Semitic languages, shows signs of being originally a constructed language. It is built up upon mathematical principles—phenomena not paralleled by any other language." (Cleary 1998).*

The description of the natural world in the Koran pre-empts much of today's hard-earned scientific findings (see http://www.rationalreality.com). Consistent with Karl Popper's *Critical Rationalism*, the Koran offers falsification. As such it challenges people of learning to find fault with it and to falsify it. By discovering the Koran, I had unlocked the key to the reality of my 'life-world' within the context of a natural social order, natured in humankind. Sociobiology and neurology are coming close to confirming the "God" part of the brain, "natured" in humankind (Koran 30:30). We live in exciting times. In the intellectual world, the Koran, the source of Islam, presents itself as a challenge to human explanation.

> "They only know some appearances of the life-world, yet of the ultimate end they are heedless." (Koran 30:7)

Bibliography:

Asadi, Muhammed. *Rational Reality* (www.rationalreality.com)
Asadi, Muhammed. *The Justice Paradigm* (http://www.geocities.com/justiceparadigm).
Koran: Translated from the Arabic
Babbie, Earl. *The Practice of Social Research.* 6th ed. 1992. Wadsworth Publishing Co. California.
Chinyelu, Mamadou. *Harlem Ain't Nothin' But a Third World Country.* 1999. Mustard Seed Press. New York
Cleary, Thomas. *Koran: The Heart of Islam.* 1998.
Ed. Shafritz & Ott. Editors. *The Classics of Organization Theory.* 2000.
Mills. C Wright. *The Power Elite.* 1956.
Schaefer, Robert T & Lamm Robert P. *Sociology.* 6th ed. New York. McGraw Hill Companies.
Zahoor, Dr. A. Ibn Khaldun. [http://users.erols.com/zenithco/khaldun.html] retrieved 10/13/'01

THE HADITH CONSPIRACY & THE HIJACKING OF ISLAM

> "And they scattered not, those to whom was given the Book [Koran], except <u>AFTER</u> the clear sign came unto them. They had been commanded only to serve God, making their religion pure for Him alone…This indeed is the established order"
> (Koran 98:1-8)

The Koran and the History of Religion:

> *Humankind were one community, then God sent prophets as bearers of good news and as warners and revealed with them the Book with the truth that it [the Book] might judge between humankind concerning that in which they differed. And only those to whom the book was given differed concerning it, after clear proofs had been given them, through mutual hatred and rivalry…(Koran 2:213)*

Hadith are the various traditions contained in specific books, believed in by the majority of Muslims to be the sayings of the prophet Muhammed. These in the major part are extra-Koranic, i.e. from outside the Koran. They either contradict or add to the Koran. Muslims sometimes present them as an explanation of the Koran or as an integral part of Islamic law, even though the Koran does not confirm them.

A minority among the Muslims does not accept the various books of *Hadith* as being an accurate representation of what the prophet

Muhammed said. They take the Koran as Criterion (*Furqaan* in Arabic), according to the Koran's own claim (2:185), accepting only those *Hadith* [tradition or narration attributed to the prophet], which the Koran confirms and attests in totality. I represent that view in this writing. Opposition to the *Hadith*, and the whole body of extra-Koranic literature on Islam as doctrine has existed from the earliest days of Islam. This is well documented by Shafi (died 204AH/819AD). The Koran historically predates any written *Hadith* and there is no mention of *Hadith* or the *Sunna* of the Prophet [practice of the prophet] in what we possess as writings before the third century after the prophet. Koran and rationality based on its principles formed the basis of religion for first century Muslims (Rahman 1979). Thus contrary to being an innovation, following the Koran alone is historically the original Islam and *Hadith* and other extra-Koranic literature is an innovation, introduced in its written form in the 3rd century after the prophet.

> "And they scattered not, those who were given the Book, except AFTER the clear sign came unto them. They were commanded only to serve God, making the way PURE for Him alone..." (Koran 98:1-)

<u>Hadith and the Gospels:</u>

The various books of *Hadith* that we see in Muslim society today are the same in relation to Muhammed, as the Gospels are to Jesus. They are both similar in that both were complied [in what we possess today] centuries after Muhammed and Jesus respectively [unlike the Koran which was memorized and written down at the time of its revelation] and they both present no proof of authenticity [unlike the Koran in which numerous verses say: In this is a sign (or proof)..." and then asks you to refute it]. Therefore, objectively speaking both the *Hadith* and the Gospels do not present any evidence as to be considered a 100% reliable representation of the words of the prophets, Muhammad and Jesus. Modern scholarship of both the Gospels [the Jesus Seminar] and the *Hadith* finds them an unreliable representation of the words of the prophets or even their close companions.

Fazlur Rahman, who was the Harold H. Swift Distinguished Service Professor of Islamic Thought at the University of Chicago, wrote in his book *Islam* (1966) on the historic study of the *Hadith*. Summarising I. Goldziher's scientific study of the *Hadith*, he writes:

> "But his argument runs, since the corpus of the Hadith continued to swell in each succeeding generation, and since in each generation the material runs parallel to and reflects various and often contradictory doctrines of Muslim theological and legal schools, the final recorded product of the Hadith, which date from the $3^{rd}/9^{th}$ century [over 250 years after the death of the prophet], must be regarded as being on the whole <u>unreliable</u> as a source for the prophets own teaching and conduct." (1979:44)

Professor Schacht, who according to Fazlur Rahman is the first scholar to have undertaken an "extensive and systematic comparison of legal traditions in their historical sequence, is unassailably scientific and sound in method...(1979:47-48), did not believe that the *Hadith* or the concept of "*Sunna* of the Prophet" were part of first century Islam. Shafi [150-204/767-819] introduced them, at the earliest, nearly two hundred years after the death of the prophet. The Koran states exactly the same. The Koran was the only "*Hadith*" that was conveyed by the prophet and formed the guidance for the early Muslim community.

Most Muslims who have taken on themselves the responsibility of teaching Islam to others have themselves abandoned the Koran by upholding *Hadith*. They say without hesitation: *"The majority of Shariah (Law) in Islam is contained outside the Koran in books of Hadith and fiqh."* Such a saying is a direct attack on the validity of the Koran, which claims to contain the complete Islamic law from God. We need to ask ourselves, what kind of submission (Islam) is this when you are rejecting God's words to follow your traditions?

> "...If any do fail to judge by what Allah (God) has sent down (i.e. the Koran), they are unbelievers (Kaafiroon)." (Koran 5:45).
> "...If any do fail to judge by that which Allah has sent down, they are tyrants (dhilamoon)." (Koran 5:45)
> "...If any do fail to judge by that which Allah has sent down, such are evil-livers (fasikoon)." (Koran 5:47)

The Koran reports that the messenger himself will complain to God about his so-called followers abandoning the Koran:

> "And the messenger says,"O my Lord, <u>my OWN</u> people have forsaken the Koran." (Koran 25:30)

Muslims, those who claim also to believe in the *Hadith* as being totally true, need to be objective and not subjective. They should, as concern for truth demands, not change standards while evaluating phenomena. If they reject the Gospels as being true based on reasons that are valid, i.e. contradictions, history etc (and they almost all do), then they should also reject the *Hadith* on the same criteria. *Hadith* have the same problems of authenticity as the Gospels do. *Hadith* do not represent the words of Muhammed just like the Gospels do not represent the words of Jesus, in total.

> "One would be mistaken in thinking that once the Gospels were written they constituted the basic Scriptures of the newly born Christianity and that people referred to them the same way they referred to the Old Testament. At that time, the foremost authority was the oral tradition as a vehicle for Jesus' words and the teachings of the apostles. The first writings to circulate were Paul's letters and they occupied a prevalent position long before the Gospels. They were, after all, written several decades earlier.
> It has already been shown that contrary to what certain commentators are still writing today, before 140 AD there was no witness to the knowledge that a collection of Gospel writings

existed. It was not until circa 170 AD that the four Gospels acquired the status of canonic literature." (Bucaille 1987).

Both the *Hadith* and the Gospels are based on oral traditions that were written down, in the written form that we have today, centuries after the prophets, Muhammed and Jesus. In recalling events, a gap of even a year can be distorted by memory beyond recognition. However, when the gap is of more than a hundred years, and you are narrating something to support a point of view [the Ahl-al Kalam and Mutizila, against the Ahl al *Hadith* in early Islam or the Judeo Christians against the Pauline Christians in early Christianity], your own as against conflicting points of view, the distortions are immense. Since history shows that eventually the followers of the *Hadith* and the followers of Pauline Christianity, politically dominated the scene both the teachings of Muhammed and Jesus got distorted. Modern scholarship recognizes this. Except for the Koran, we have no reliable historical record of the message that Muhammed conveyed.

John Dominic Crossan, in his book, *The Birth of Christianity (1998)*, cites a study done after the Challenger explosion:

"The morning after the Challenger explosion, the 106 students in Psychology 101 [Personality Development] at Emory University filled out questionnaires on how they had first heard of the disaster. That established a baseline for their memories within twenty-four hours of the even itself in January of 1986. Then in October of 1988, the forty-four of 106 students still at Emory were requestioned (only 25% remembered the original questionnaire) and their two answers compared. Finally in March of 1989, follow up interviews were given to the forty students willing to participate in the final phase of the experiment...When those second versions were compared with the first ones for accuracy and graded on a 0-7 scale for major and minor attributes of the event, the mean was a 2.95 out of a possible 7. Eleven subjects

were wrong about everything and scored 0 (25% of the sample). Twenty two of them [50% of the sample] scored 2 or less, this means that if they were right on one major attribute, they were wrong on both of the others...what makes these low scores interesting is the high degree of confidence that accompanied many of them." (Crossan 1998: 62-63)

The Koran captures the similarity of what has happened in the case of both Jesus and Muhammed in this statement:

"Has not the time arrived for the believers that their hearts should engage in the admonishment from God and the truth that has been revealed to them and that they should not become like those to whom was given the Book before, but long ages passed over them and their hearts grew hard.."(Koran 57:16)

Hadith believing Muslims make big claims on the so-called scientific compilation of *Hadith*. Let it be clear however, that no matter how scientific you are in your compilation of what is "false" to start with, the compilation cannot make it true. Even the criteria that are presented are subjective, i.e. the truthfulness of a particular narrator with a story of how truthful he was. To repeat, falsehood is not converted to truth by its scientific compilation. The scientific method demands that "subjective" proof i.e. how truthful a person was, be ignored and the item tested on objective criteria. What does the content say?

THE DILEMMA:

Hadith doctors have traditionally evaluated *Hadith* on its chain of narrators and its body text, according to their own criteria of what should be correct. However even according to their own standards, they fell into a dilemma. Some *Hadith* exist which have, according to them, a "sound" chain of narrators i.e. it was truthfully narrated but they dispute the text of the *Hadith*. A single example of this (and there are many) and the whole system collapses. The Koran gives us the standard for judging anything that is presented on Islam. If the Koran confirms it in total it's true Islam. If the material adds to or contradicts the Koran, its source is neither God nor his messenger. The unreliable nature of the collection of the oral *Hadith*, i.e. x said that y said that z heard that l, m, n, o, p conveyed that they heard someone narrate from the prophet such and so, is a type of flimsy "evidence" that would not stand up as true in any civilized court of law in any country.

HISTORY OF COMPILATION OF HADITH:

Out of the books that the majority of Muslims believe in as being authentic, Sahih Bukhari is presented as being the MOST authentic. However an analysis of the history of the books shows that it is anything but authentic. Bokhari, the collector of the narration lived in a period over 230 years after the death of the prophet. Out of the 600,000 *Hadith* (narrations) that he collected, which were initially attributed to the prophet, he threw out as fabrication 592,700 of them and kept only 7300 as being genuine. They further reduce to 2762 *Hadith* after removing repetition.

The margin of error in these numbers is so great, that any rational inquirer can see that accepting the book of Bukhari as containing all authentic *Hadith* or even a majority of authentic *Hadith* is stupidity. Yet the majority of Muslims unquestionable accept it as "Gospel" truth!

There are many scientific and logical errors and contradictions in the Book of Bukhari, as well as the other books. Some examples:

1. The prophet according to Bukhari in one of the narration tells his companion Abu—Dharr Ghafari that the sun goes around the earth, in the apparent description that he gives (*Hadith* 421, pg. 283, vol. 4 of M.Muhsin Khan's translation of Sahih Bukhari).

This erroneous view was very popular at the time Bukhari compiled his collection. However it is absurd. We know today that the earth revolves around the sun, proven by scientific evidence. The Koran not only corrected this erroneous notion but also gave an accurate description of a round earth.

2. According to *Hadith* no disease is contagious [*Adwa*]. This, as we all know, is inaccurate. What about the common cold and viruses like Ebola etc [*Hadith* 649, page 435, volume7].

3. Books of *Hadith* contain many home-remedies, according to ideas prevalent at that time, which are scientifically absurd. The *Hadith* mentions there being a cure for every ailment in black cumin seed [*Hadith* 591, pg.400, vol. 7]. This is evidently not true. Can it cure cancer or AIDS, not to mention even the common cold? *Hadith* suggests that we drink "camel-urine" to recuperate after an illness [*Hadith* 590, pg.399, vol.7]. This is not only disgusting, but urine is toxic stuff that the body discards to protect itself from harm. The Koran places extreme importance on cleanliness and clean eating (*tayyab*).

4. The famous *Hadith* about the fly: *"If a fly falls into the vessel of any of you, let him dip all of it (in the vessel) and then throw it away [and use the material in the vessel], for in one of its wings there is a disease and in the other there is a healing [Bukhari, Hadith 673, pg. 452, vol. 7]*

If people took the above as "*Hadith*-truth", just like "Gospel truth", preventable deaths from disease like cholera and typhoid would definitely go up.

5. According to Bukhari 56/152 and Hanbel 3/107, 163; the prophet recommended that people drink camel urine to recuperate after an illness Later on when the same people killed the prophet's shepherd, he commanded that they be seized, their eyes taken out and their hands and feet cut and left them thirsty in the desert. This does not fit in with the personality of the prophet presented in the Koran. The Koran says that the prophet was compassionate towards the people he encountered. How could the prophet recommend the drinking of camel's urine, considering the importance that the Koran places on hygiene?

6. The Koran commands believers not to make any distinction between any of God's messengers (Koran 2:285 and many other places), yet according to Bukhari's books of *Hadith* (Bukhari 97/36), the prophet contradicted the Koran saying that he was the "most honor-

able" among all the messengers. Not only this, the books of Bukhari make the prophet even contradict himself by saying in a different *Hadith* (Bukhari 65/4,6 and Hanbel 1/205,242,440) that we should not make any distinction between the messengers and that he was not better than even Yunus (Jonah), who disobeyed God. Could the prophet have contradicted the Koran? Could the prophet of Allah have contradicted himself? These are questions that traditional Muslims who accept the Hadith need to answer.

7. According to the books of *Hadith*, a woman is compared to a black dog or a monkey (this *Hadith* pre-dates Darwin but it refers to women only) Bukhari 8/102 and Hanbel 4/86. The Koran on the other hand honors women and lifts up their status, contrary to the *Hadith*. A woman is called bad luck in the *Hadith* (Bukhari 76/53). Also, according to the collection of Muslim (Sahih Muslim), most of the people in hell were of the feminine gender! According to Bukhari, "Women are naturally, morally and religiously defective." Therefore, according to the standard of the Koran, no Muslim should accept such prejudiced *Hadith* as issuing from the lips of the prophet of God. They have nothing to do with Islam.

8. According to Bukhari (Book of Jihad, 146) and Abu Dawd 113, the prophet gave permission to warriors to kill women and children in war. Indeed these people, who have hijacked Islam, are attributing tyranny to a prophet held in honor by Allah, and described as having mercy for the people. The Koran says, even about the people that attack us first, that we should quit fighting if they offer peace, leave alone killing women and children. According to the standard of the Koran, the prophet could <u>never</u> have asked his warriors to kill women and children. The dignity of every single human life, be it male or female, of whatever race, nationality or religion, given by the Koran is unsurpassed in world literature, past or present. The Koran states explicitly that killing even one innocent individual is as if the whole of humanity is killed (Koran 5:32).

9. The Koran describes accurately the shape of the earth as being rounded (Koran 39:5), and the cause of night and day as being the rotation of the earth. The *Hadith* and similar writings however contain mythological concepts, which are then by hook or by crook attributed to the prophet. The most famous commentary of the Koran, that by Ibn Kathir (2/29 and 50/1) makes extensive use of the *Hadith* in explaining the Koran. In that spirit, Ibn Kathir suggests that the earth is "carried on a giant bull." When the bull shakes its head, an earthquake results. As stated earlier, Bukhari's book of *Hadith* states that the sun revolves around the earth.

10. According to Hanbel 4/85, 5/54, the prophet ordered that all black dogs be killed because they were devils. Inspired by that *Hadith,* so called "Muslims" kill hundreds of dogs all over the world and consider them unclean. The Koran, contrary to that, talks about the sleepers in the cave (chapter 18) having a dog, inside their dwelling place and allows meat killed by hunting dogs. There is nothing in the Koran which even remotely suggests that dogs are unclean rather than useful animals.

11. The Koran states that," *Vision cannot comprehend God, who comprehends all vision,*" yet the *Hadith* of Bukhari 97/24 and 10/129 says that to prove his identity to Muhammed, God showed the prophet his shin.

12. The *Hadith*, in complete opposition to the Koran mentions, "stoning to death," as the punishment for adultery in the case of married couples. This is completely against the commandments of the Koran (Koran 24:1-5). This *Hadith* is borrowed from a similar ruling in the Old Testament. It contradicts the Koran. Could the prophet have issued a ruling contrary to the ruling of Allah in the Koran?

The Koran suggests halving or doubling the punishment for adultery, based on circumstance. How can you kill someone (stone to death) half or double, is another question that Muslims who believe in the Hadith need to answer?

13. The Koran talks of itself as being the only message that God intended the prophet to convey (Koran 42:52, 14:52; 69:44; 6:19 etc.). The *Hadith* of Muslim quotes the prophet as saying (Muslim, Zuhd 72, Hanbel 3/12,21,39) that no one should write anything from him other than the Koran. This particular *Hadith* is in harmony with the Koran, but then another *Hadith* contradicts not only the Koran but this *Hadith* as well. The prophet is quoted as asking, in Hanbel 2/162, *Amr bin As*, his companion to write everything he spoke.

14. The Koran states that those who forbid things even though God has allowed them, are committing a great transgression. Yet the followers of *Hadith* have forbidden (i.e. made *haraam*) the use of silk and gold by men, even though the Koran does not forbid their use. Contrary to that they are specifically mentioned as being permissible keeping within the boundaries set by God (Koran 7:30-32, 42:21; 22:23; 35:33). The *Hadith* in keeping with its reputation of contradictions, even contradicts this forbidding law by stating that the prophet allowed a "gold ring" to be worn by one of his companions and forbade the others! Could the prophet have invented laws not in the Koran? Could he then have been partial in implementing those laws? Those who have hijacked Islam need to answer these questions.

15. The Koran only prohibits the meat of one animal, the pig. Certain sects in Islam however, based on the authority of the *Hadith* forbid clams, shrimp, crab etc. Why are they attributing against God a lie if they are submitters?

The Koran claims to be the best *Hadith* (Ahsan ul *Hadith* 39:23), and states that after Allah and his ayat (verses) no other *Hadith* is to be followed (Koran 45:6). The Koran also states that people have fabricated *Hadith* to mislead from the way of Allah (Koran 31:6 Lahwal *Hadith*). The Koran challenges people to produce a "*Hadith*" like the Koran (Koran 52:34) if they are truthful. The difference in language, style and content between the Koran and the other "*Hadith*" has been evident and is not denied even by those who believe in the *Hadith* as being genuine.

> "These are the verses of Allah (God) which we rehearse to you with truth. Then in what Hadith will they believe after Allah and His verses?" (Koran 45:6).

The Koran's Verdict:

> "And the messenger says of Judgment Day, "O my Lord! My own people took this Koran as a thing to be shunned (KORAN 25:30)."

According to the Koran, as has been the case in the history of all the prophets (Koran 25:30-33), Muslims have fallen victim to inventions against the Koran. These inventions have distorted the way that God sent down via all the prophets. The message that God has been sending down has been the same throughout history, same in every way (Koran 42: 13). Even though the Koran says in well over 15 places, that it is explained in detail, *Tafseel* (Koran 6:114 etc.), and contains a full explanation of whatever is needed by a believer (Koran 16:89), and should be enough, *Kaafi*, for them (Koran 29:51), and contains the complete law (*Shariah*) of God (Koran 45:18 and 42:13), as against man-made law or *Shariah* (Koran 42:21), "Muslims" insist that the Koran needs supplements to be understood, and lacks details. This amounts to disbelieving what God himself says in unequivocal terms in the Koran.

The Koran and Hadith:

The Koran states explicitly that the messenger's duty was only to convey (*Balagh*) the message (Koran 29:18) contained in the Koran (Koran 69:44) and that the Koran was the only *Wahi* (revelation) given to the prophet to be conveyed to people (Koran 6:19), by testimony of God Himself. Therefore to follow the words of God in the Koran would be to follow the messenger (see Koran 4:80).

These inventions against the words of God, revealed to the messengers, which is called their true speech (*Qawl*—Koran 69:40), are the so-called "*Hadith*" or so-called stories about the sayings and doings of the prophets. Such stories can be found in the Old Testament, the Gospels of Jesus (i.e. the "*Hadith*" about Jesus), and the various *Hadith* about the prophet Muhammed contained in the many "extra-Koranic" books believed in by the *Sunni* and *Shia* schools of thought. People have attributed these things throughout history to the messengers, whereas the messengers could never have said them given the history of the documents and the Criterion (*Furqaan*) of the Koran (Koran 2:185)

The Koran states:

> "Do they not consider the Koran with care, If it had been from anyone other than Allah, it would contain many discrepancies." (Koran 4:82)

Any document that claims to be from God, but in actuality is not would contain some form of error according to the Koran. What we see on analysis is that the *Hadith* attributed to Muhammed and the Gospels attributed to Jesus fail this test of authenticity. What we also see is the subjectivity of the various Muslims groups. They reject the Gospels of Jesus based on the same test as being corrupt whereas they overlook similar defects found in the books of Hadith and they accept them as being authentic sayings of Muhammed.

The Koran says in well over 15 places that it is "explained in detail" (6:114 etc). One word used is *Tafseel*, which means a detailed explanation. It further says that it contains a *Biyan* or clear exposition of everything (16:89). God says in the Koran that He neglected nothing in the Book (6:38). The Koran talks about Moses' Book being *Tamam* (which means complete), and that the Koran is in no way less than that. The Koran also suggests that it should be *Kaafi* meaning "enough" for guidance by itself (29:51).

The Koran states explicitly that the messenger's duty was *only "to convey the message (29:18),"* and he said nothing on his own as his own sayings (69:44). It states that the message that the messenger conveyed was the Koran only (42:52 & 14:52 & 69:44). Therefore, to follow God's words in the Koran would be to follow the messenger, (4:80), as the words of the Koran are the messenger's speech (*Qawl*—69:40). The Koran claims that it contains answers to ALL relevant questions (25:33) and contains the best explanation (*Tafseer*) of itself (25:33 & 2:159). The Koran claims to be the *Hukm* or commandments of God, according to which humankind is to be judged (5:48). It also states that it is the *Shariah* or law/way with which God sent the messenger (45:18 & 42:13). Who would know best on how to talk to humankind but their creator? Therefore, it makes no sense to say that outside sources better explain God's word.

In Koran 2:185 it is stated explicitly that the Koran is the Criterion (*Furqaan*). It is the distinguisher between what is correct and what is wrong. If the Koran is missing details, as Muslim sects purport, how can it be a criterion or a distinguisher over those details?

Notes and References:

The Koran is in detail [6:114; 2:159-160; 10:37; 11:11; 41:1-3; 22:16; 6:38; 12:111; 14:52; 17:89; 75:16-19; 18:54; 20:113; 39:27-28; 54:17; 25:33; 16:89 etc.]

The messenger's duty is only to convey the Book [5:102; 16:35; 16:82; 24:54; 36:16-17; 14:52 etc.]

The way sent down by God has been uniform in history in every way [41:43; 42:13; 46:9; 30:30; 6:20; 23:68; 21:24; 4:26; 1:7 read together with 19:58; 6:83-88]

Extra-Koranic *Hadith* an innovation [6:112; 22:52; 17:73-77; 10:15; 16:116; 42:21; 10:69-70; 5:47-49; 7:28; 33:64-68; 6:123; 6:144; 49:16; 39:23; 45:6; 31:6; 52:33-34; 31:20; 6:116; 2:170; 69:38-49; 81:15-19; 51:7-11]

Bibliography:

1. Koran. Translated from the Arabic
2. The Bible. Revised Standard Version (1971)
3. Fazlur Rahman. Islam (1979). University of Chicago Press. Chicago. Illinois.
4. Sahih Al Bokhari. English Translation by M. Muhsin Khan.
5. References to the Koran in this paper e.g. 39:23 refer to Koran chapter or sura 39, aya or verse 23. References to the various books of *Hadith* e.g. Bukhari 56/152 refer to the Book of Bukhari, book (chapter) 56, *Hadith* number 152.

THE UNIFYING THEORY OF EVERYTHING

"The Nature of God according to which He has originated humankind..." (Koran 30:30)

The document containing the natural order is the Koran. God conveyed it to humankind through his messengers. Muhammed was the last of God's prophets. The prophet is not held to be the author of the Koran, but only an emissary and witness who gives warning and announces good news [48:8]; the words of the Koran—God's own words are fully distinct from Muhammed's words [75:16-18; 53:3-5; 69:44-46; 87:6; 73:5], for the revelation forces itself upon his consciousness from without, coming unexpectedly upon him [42:51-52]. Muhammed was a man, a mortal, God's messenger [3:144; 41:6].

The Divine message, completely clear [44:2] is revealed to God's messengers by God's command. It was revealed on a "blessed night [44:2]", the "Night of Power [97:1-]." It is a "Mighty Book [41:41]," "completely overpowering [59:21]," which is sent down as something preexisting [20:99; 27:6], in the "protected tablet [85:21]," that is the core of the book [43:3] and embodies God's eternal knowledge and judgment of all things [34:3], the total content of which is too great to be contained in any material document [18:108]. Ultimately, God's universal dominion is manifested in all things, and even the simplest processes of nature are signs or tokens (*ayah*) of His being one and His creative power.

> *"In whatever direction you turn there is the face of God [2:115]"*
> *"God is closer to man [woman] than their own jugular vein [50:15]."*

God manifests his signs within the immediacy of consciousness and in the horizons of the created world [41:53].

> *"And it the earth are signs for those who are sure and within yourselves. Can you not see? And by the Cherisher [God] of the heavens and earth it is the truth just as the fact that you converse [51:20-21]."*

He [God] shows himself in the simple alteration of night and day [36:37etc] and in the stages of growth of humans from conception to birth to senility and death [23:12-16; 40:67]. In all things there is evidence of God's being for those "who can see [24:44]," who will, "reflect, ponder and understand [45:13; 16:11-13]," and will perhaps show gratitude and be guided aright [16:11-15]. His signs are effective for those who have opened themselves to Him with certainty [45:1-4; 10:6]; but this opening and receptivity to God's grace is ultimately worked by God himself based on justice, to those who deserve it [39:23; 2:26; 39:17-18].

The revelation of the Koran was a gratuitous act of mercy and blessing towards humans [45:20; 29:51, 44:2-8]. God sends His messengers [*rasul*] and prophets [*nabiyyin*] with the Book, wherein His signs are set forth explicitly and unequivocally and the standard order of the Universe is explained [11:1, 10:38; 41:1], as a guidance, admonition, healing and a criterion to differentiate between right and wrong, truth and falsehood [10:57; 2:185]. It is an admonition—a calling to mind [20:99] of His power, justice and mercy. A warning of impeding judgment based on His absolute justice [6:17-20; 82:6-19; 98:1-8; 88:1-26 etc.]. It is a call to worship God alone [6:102; 3:1-3], and to live according to the norms of justice and morality demanded and decreed by Him.

The signs [verses] of the Book are the signs par excellence, for it is throughout them that all other signs are brought to the attention of humans and made intelligible. It is thus the unifying **"Theory of**

Everything." Recited by God's messengers, the signs are self-expressing in that they address themselves immediately to the understanding of the hearer in the clear form of articulate language. This is in contrast to worldly and self centered desires [*al-ahwa*] and conjectures [*zann*] of humans, which deceives people away from God [28:50; 10:36-39].

The Koran is given by God Himself and is taught and explained by Him [53:3-5; 55:1-5; 69:40-43; 75:16-19]. In it lies knowledge based on true reality [30:56; 29:49;34:6] as opposed to mere human opinion [10:36-39]. It is the Creator's truth, the visible truth that destroys the vanity of untruth [17:81-82; 8:6], being the manifestation of God who is the ultimate truth [10:32-36; 22:6; 22:62]. It is the light that God gives to whom He wills [42:52] based on justice, wherein and whereby humans should be guided [57:9; 2:185], to God the source who is the "light of the heavens and the earth [24:35]." As a result the true believers, when they hear the signs, verses of the Koran, fall prostrate and glorify God, their eyes overflowing with tears [7:119-122; 32:15].

In the Koran, God reveals Himself by His attributes and names, and thereby, since He is the maker of all creation, He makes manifest to the believer the true nature, the standard order [30:30] of created existence [*deen al qiyamma*].

According to the Koran, the response of humans to God's words ought to be immediate, for God created them and designed their powers of perception and understanding [32:9; 16:78; 67:23 etc.]. At the very foundation of their being, in the standard order of things, lies a testimony that God is their Cherisher, Lord [7:171].

Through the messengers, God calls humanity to submit to Him completely, worshipping Him alone and living according to His law; the creator's law best fitting the needs of His creation [67:14]. Humans according to the Koran, however are too frequently distracted by their engagement in the pursuit of the goods of the world [10:7-9; 30:7, etc.], being seduced by their competition in the "ornaments of this life,[64:14-15 etc.]. They are by their nature anxious [41:49-51; 17:19-23 etc] and do not look beyond their material existence [45:24-26 etc].

The Koran recognizes that importance of a number of sociological factors that blind men to God's message—Group solidarity, tradition etc [7:28; 7:70; 9:24; 6:108; 43:22-23 etc.] and the obstinate pride in social position that characterizes those who refuse God's signs [74:11-30 etc.]. This is in contrast to the attitude of the sincere [21:19-21] who are willing to abandon these things for the sake of truth and God [12:207].

The insensibility to God's signs and the preaching of His word appears in a kind of intellectual blindness 18:21-24; 2:18 etc.], realized in a constant obstinacy and refusal to perceive and reflect. People's perseverance in this refusal to accept God's guidance is ultimately ratified and made permanent by God, who so "seals the hearts [63:3 etc.], that regardless of what the messengers say or do, they will never believe [36:9-10 etc.].

God grants His mercy and guidance to whomsoever He wills, based on justice [24:46; 6:125, etc]. If He wished, all humans would believe [32:13 etc.], for all creatures are under God's immediate providence. He refuses however, to guide the unjust and the sinful and those who refuse Him [9:37; 9:109; 40:28 etc]. God's judgment is based on justice. The Koran states that God is not unjust in the least. He does not wrong humankind but humankind "wrong themselves." It says that punishment will be according to the harm done and not more or less in the least, if it is not forgiven based on effort [16:111; 16:118; 3:117; 10:44]. The Koran states that God has nothing to gain by punishing, if people were to do right [4:147] and the consequence of wrong has ill effect on society and harms the multitude [30:41]. The punishment of wrong will be based on God's absolute justice, for this life is but a test of people's goodness and justice [67:2; 18:7; 21:35]. God demands no more than what a person is capable of [2:286; 7:42, etc.], for He is the Most Forgiving, the Most Merciful and the Most Just.

Acknowledgement:

The above section on the Koran was adapted and modified from, "Qur'an," *The New Catholic Encyclopedia, volume 8. The Catholic University of America. 1967.*

"We, who are children of the Universe—animated stardust—can nevertheless **reflect** on the nature of that same Universe…How we have become linked into this <u>cosmic dimension</u> is a mystery. Yet the linkage cannot be denied…Through conscious beings the Universe has generated self-awareness. This can be no trivial detail, no minor byproduct of mindless, purposeless forces. We are truly meant to be here."
(Physicist Paul Davies, The Mind of God, 1992)

"Do they not **reflect** within <u>themselves</u>? God did not create the <u>skies and the earth</u> and that which is between them but for truth, and (for) an appointed term."
(Koran 30:8)

0-595-12904-8

Printed in the United States
971200005B